UNLOCK

READING & WRITING SKILLS

4

Johanna Stirling

CAMBRIDGE
UNIVERSITY PRESS

CAMBRIDGE
UNIVERSITY PRESS

University Printing House, Cambridge CB2 8BS, United Kingdom

Cambridge University Press is part of the University of Cambridge.

It furthers the University's mission by disseminating knowledge in the pursuit of education, learning and research at the highest international levels of excellence.

www.cambridge.org
Information on this title: www.cambridge.org/9781107614093

© Cambridge University Press 2014

First published 2014

Printed in Dubai by Oriental Press

A catalogue record for this publication is available from the British Library

ISBN 978-1-107-61525-0 Reading and Writing 4 Student's Book with Online Workbook
ISBN 978-1-107-61409-3 Reading and Writing 4 Teacher's Book with DVD
ISBN 978-1-107-63461-9 Listening and Speaking 4 Student's Book with Online Workbook
ISBN 978-1-107-65052-7 Listening and Speaking 4 Teacher's Book with DVD

Additional resources for this publication at www.cambridge.org/unlock

CONTENTS

Introduction   4

Teaching tips   9

UNIT 1   Globalization   12

UNIT 2   Education   20

UNIT 3   Medicine   28

UNIT 4   Risk   37

UNIT 5   Manufacturing   45

UNIT 6   Environment   53

UNIT 7   Architecture   61

UNIT 8   Energy   69

UNIT 9   Art and design   77

UNIT 10   Ageing   84

Review tests answer key   92

Review tests   95

Additional Writing tasks and model answers   125

Acknowledgements   135

UNL⌀CK UNIT STRUCTURE

The units in *Unlock Reading & Writing Skills* are carefully scaffolded so that students are taken step-by-step through the writing process.

UNLOCK YOUR KNOWLEDGE | Encourages discussion around the theme of the unit with inspiration from interesting questions and striking visuals.

WATCH AND LISTEN | Features an engaging and motivating *Discovery Education™* video which generates interest in the topic.

READING 1 | Practises the reading skills required to understand academic texts as well as the vocabulary needed to comprehend the text itself.

READING 2 | Presents a second text which provides a different angle on the topic in a different genre. It is a model text for the writing task.

LANGUAGE DEVELOPMENT | Practises the vocabulary and grammar from the Readings in preparation for the writing task.

CRITICAL THINKING | Contains brainstorming, evaluative and analytical tasks as preparation for the writing task.

GRAMMAR FOR WRITING | Presents and practises grammatical structures and features needed for the writing task.

ACADEMIC WRITING SKILLS | Practises all the writing skills needed for the writing task.

WRITING TASK | Uses the skills and language learnt over the course of the unit to draft and edit the writing task. Requires students to produce a piece of academic writing. Checklists help learners to edit their work.

OBJECTIVES REVIEW | Allows students to assess how well they have mastered the skills covered in the unit.

WORDLIST | Includes the key vocabulary from the unit.

This is the unit's main learning objective. It gives learners the opportunity to use all the language and skills they have learnt in the unit.

UNL**O**CK YOUR KNOWLEDGE

Work with a partner. Discuss the questions below.

1 Look at your clothes, the items on your desk, in your bag and pockets. Where were they made? How many were made in your country?
2 Does it matter that we now import so many goods from other countries? Why? / Why not?
3 What effects has globalization had on your country?

PERSONALIZE

Unlock encourages students to bring their own knowledge, experiences and opinions to the topics. This motivates students to relate the topics to their own contexts.

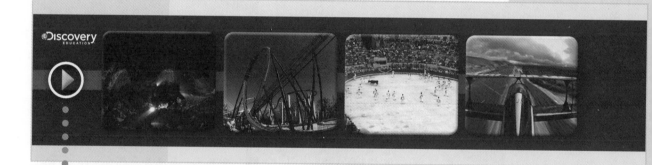

DISCOVERY EDUCATION™ VIDEO

Thought-provoking videos from *Discovery Education™* are included in every unit throughout the course to introduce topics, promote discussion and motivate learners. The videos provide a new angle on a wide range of academic subjects.

> The video was excellent! It helped with raising students' interest in the topic. It was well-structured and the language level was appropriate.
>
> Maria Agata Szczerbik,
> United Arab Emirates University,
> Al-Ain, UAE

UNL⊘CK CRITICAL THINKING

> " The Critical thinking sections present a difficult area in an engaging and accessible way.
>
> Shirley Norton, London School of English, UK "

BLOOM'S TAXONOMY

CREATE — create, invent, plan, compose, construct, design, imagine

decide, rate, choose, recommend, justify, assess, prioritize — **EVALUATE**

ANALYZE — explain, contrast, examine, identify, investigate, categorize

show, complete, use, classify, examine, illustrate, solve — **APPLY**

UNDERSTAND — compare, discuss, restate, predict, translate, outline

name, describe, relate, find, list, write, tell — **REMEMBER**

BLOOM'S TAXONOMY

The Critical Thinking sections in *Unlock* are based on Benjamin Bloom's classification of learning objectives. This ensures learners develop their **lower-** and **higher-order thinking skills**, ranging from demonstrating **knowledge** and **understanding** to in-depth **evaluation**.
The margin headings in the Critical Thinking sections highlight the exercises which develop Bloom's concepts.

LEARN TO THINK

Learners engage in **evaluative** and **analytical tasks** that are designed to ensure they do all of the thinking and information-gathering required for the end-of-unit writing task.

CRITICAL THINKING

At the end of this unit, you will write the first draft of an essay. Look at this unit's writing task in the box below.

> How have food and eating habits changed in your country? Suggest some reasons for the changes.

UNDERSTAND

Providing supporting examples

In academic writing, you need to justify and give supporting examples to any statements or opinions that you write, to show that they are true.

UNL**O**CK RESEARCH

THE CAMBRIDGE LEARNER CORPUS 👁

The **Cambridge Learner Corpus** is a bank of official Cambridge English exam papers. Our exclusive access means we can use the corpus to carry out unique research and identify the most common errors learners make. That information is used to ensure the *Unlock* syllabus teaches the most **relevant language**.

THE WORDS YOU NEED

Language Development sections provide vocabulary and grammar building tasks that are further practised in the **UNLOCK ONLINE** Workbook. The glossary and end-of-unit wordlists provide definitions, pronunciation and handy summaries of all the key vocabulary.

GLOBALIZATION   UNIT 1

👁 LANGUAGE DEVELOPMENT

EXPLANATION

Academic alternatives to phrasal verbs

When writing essays, it is important to use language which is more formal than you would use when speaking or in informal pieces of writing.

Phrasal verbs, which usually consist of a main verb followed by a particle (e.g. *up*, *on*), are less common in academic writing than in informal writing. In academic writing, phrasal verbs can often be replaced by a single word. Using these alternatives will make your writing seem more formal and academic.

GRAMMAR FOR WRITING

EXPLANATION

Noun phrases

Nouns are often combined with other words to make noun phrases. These can express a more specific idea.

Noun phrases can be made by combining nouns with:

- other nouns: *building regulations*
- relative clauses: *a building which is very old*
- prepositional phrases: *the building at the back*
- adjectives: *the tall, white building*

ACADEMIC LANGUAGE

Unique research using the **Cambridge English Corpus** has been carried out into academic language, in order to provide learners with relevant, academic vocabulary from the start (CEFR A1 and above). This addresses a gap in current academic vocabulary mapping and ensures learners are presented with carefully selected words they will find essential during their studies.

GRAMMAR FOR WRITING

The grammar syllabus is carefully designed to help learners become good writers of English. There is a strong focus on sentence structure, word agreement and referencing, which are important for **coherent** and **organized** academic writing.

> ❝ The language development is clear and the strong lexical focus is positive as learners feel they make more progress when they learn more vocabulary.
>
> Colleen Wackrow,
> Princess Nourah Bint Abdulrahman University, Al-Riyadh, Kingdom of Saudi Arabia ❞

UNLOCK SOLUTIONS

FLEXIBLE

Unlock is available in a range of print and digital components, so teachers can mix and match according to their requirements.

UNLOCK ONLINE WORKBOOKS

The UNLOCK ONLINE Workbooks are accessed via activation codes packaged with the Student's Books. These **easy-to-use** workbooks provide interactive exercises, games, tasks, and further practice of the language and skills from the Student's Books in the Cambridge LMS, an engaging and modern learning environment.

CAMBRIDGE LEARNING MANAGEMENT SYSTEM (LMS)

The Cambridge LMS provides teachers with the ability to track learner progress and save valuable time thanks to automated marking functionality. Blogs, forums and other tools are also available to facilitate communication between students and teachers.

UNLOCK EBOOKS

The *Unlock* Student's Books and Teacher's Books are also available as interactive eBooks. With answers and *Discovery Education™* videos embedded, the eBooks provide a great alternative to the printed materials.

UNLOCK TEACHING TIPS

1 Using video in the classroom

The *Watch and listen* sections in *Unlock* are based on documentary-style videos from Discovery Education™. Each one provides a fresh angle on the unit topic and a stimulating lead-in to the unit.

There are many different ways of using the video in class. For example, you could use the video for free note-taking practice and ask learners to compare their notes to the video script; or you could ask learners to reconstruct the voiceover or record their own commentary to the video. Try not to interrupt the first viewing of a new video, you can go back and watch sections again or explain things for struggling learners. You can also watch with the subtitles turned on when the learners have done all the listening comprehension work required of them.

See also: Goldstein, B. and Driver, P. (2014) *Language Learning with Digital Video* Cambridge University Press and the *Unlock* website www.cambridge.org/unlock for more ideas on using video in the classroom.

2 Teaching reading skills

Learners who aim to study at university will need to be comfortable dealing with long, complex texts. The reading texts in *Unlock Reading & Writing Skills* provide learners with practice obtaining meaning quickly from extensive texts. Discourage your learners from reading every word of a text line-by-line and instead focus on skimming and scanning:

- Skimming – help promote quick and efficient reading. Ask learners to pass quickly over the text to get the basic gist, an awareness of the organization of the text and the tone and intention of the writer.

- Scanning – help learners locate key data and reject irrelevant information in a text. Ask learners to run their eyes up, down and diagonally (from left to right) across the text looking for clusters of important words. Search for names, places, people, dates, quantities, lists of nouns and compound adjectives.

The reading texts in *Unlock Reading & Writing Skills* demonstrate different genres such as academic text, magazine article or learner essay.

The *Reading between the lines* sections make learners aware of the different conventions of each genre. Understanding text genre should help prepare learners for the kind of content to expect in the text they are going to read. Ask learners to use *Reading 2* as a writing frame to plan their sentences, paragraphs and essays for the *Writing task*.

3 Managing discussions in the classroom

There are opportunities for discussion throughout *Unlock Reading & Writing Skills*. The photographs and the *Unlock your knowledge* boxes on the first page of each unit provide the first discussion opportunity. Learners could be asked to guess what is happening in the photographs or predict what is going to happen, for example. Learners could investigate the *Unlock your knowledge* questions for homework in preparation for the lesson.

Throughout the rest of the unit, the heading *Discussion* indicates a set of questions which can be an opportunity for free speaking practice. Learners can use these questions to develop their ideas about the topic and gain confidence in the arguments they will put forward in the *Writing task*.

To maximise speaking practice, learners could complete the discussion sections in pairs. Monitor each pair to check they can find enough to say and help where necessary. Encourage learners to minimise their use of their own language and make notes of any error correction and feedback after the learners have finished speaking.

An alternative approach might be to ask learners to role-play discussions in the character of one of the people in the unit. This may free the learners from the responsibility to provide the correct answer and allow them to see an argument from another perspective.

4 Teaching writing skills

Learners work towards the *Writing task* throughout the unit by learning vocabulary and grammar relevant for the *Writing task*, and then by reading about the key issues involved in the topic. Learners gather, organise and evaluate this information in the *Critical thinking* section and use it to prepare the *Writing task*. By the time learners come to attempt the *Writing task*, they have done all the thinking required to be able to write. They can do the *Writing task* during class time or for homework. If your learners require exam practice, set the writing task as a timed test with a minimum word count which is similar to the exam the learners are training for and do the writing task in exam conditions. Alternatively, allow learners to work together in the class to do the writing task and then set the *Additional writing task* (see below) in the Teacher's Book as homework.

Task and Language Checklists

Encourage your learners to edit their written work by referring to the *Task checklist* and *Language checklist* at the end of the unit.

Model answers

The model answers in the Teacher's Book can be used in a number of ways:

- Photocopy the *Writing task* model answer and hand this to your learners when you feedback on their writing task. You can highlight useful areas of language and discourse structure to help the learners compose a second draft or write a response to the additional writing tasks.

- Use the model answer as a teaching aid in class. Photocopy the answer and cut it up into paragraphs, sentences or lines then ask learners to order it correctly.

- Use a marker pen to delete academic vocabulary, key words or functional grammar. Ask learners to replace the missing words or phrases. Learners can test each other by gapping their own model answers which they swap with their partner.

Additional writing tasks

There are ten *Additional writing tasks* in the Teacher's Book, one for each unit. These provide another opportunity to practice the skills and language learnt in the unit. They can be handed out to learners or carried out on the Online Workbook.

5 Teaching vocabulary

The *Wordlist* at the end of each unit includes topic vocabulary and academic vocabulary. There are many ways that you can work with the vocabulary. During the early units, encourage the learners to learn the new words by setting regular review tests. You could ask the learners to choose e.g. five words from the unit vocabulary to learn. You could later test your learners' use of the words by asking them to write a short paragraph incorporating the words they have learned.

Use the end-of-unit *Wordlists* and the *Glossary* at the back of the book to give extra spelling practice. Set spelling tests at the end of every unit or dictate sets of words from the glossary which follow spelling patterns or contain common diagraphs (like *th, ch, sh, ph, wh*) or prefixes and suffixes (like *al-, in-, -tion, -ful*). You could also dictate a definition from the Glossary in English or provide the words in your learner's own language to make spelling tests more challenging.

6 Using the Research projects with your class

There is an opportunity for students to investigate and explore the unit topic further in the *Research projects* which feature at the end of each unit in the Teacher's Books. These are optional activities which will allow your learners to work in groups (or individually) to discover more about a particular aspect of the topic, carry out a problem-solving activity or engage in a task which takes their learning outside the classroom.

Learners can make use of the Cambridge LMS tools to share their work with the teacher or with the class as a whole. See section 5 above and section 8 on page 11 for more ideas.

7 Using UNL⌀CK digital components: Online workbook and the Cambridge Learning Management System (LMS)

The Online Workbook provides:

- additional practice of the key skills and language covered in the Student's Book through interactive exercises. The UNL⌀CK ONLINE symbol next to a section or activity in the Student's Book means that there is additional practice of that language or skill in the Online Workbook. These exercises are ideal as homework.

- End-of-unit *Writng tasks* and *Additional writing tasks* from the Teacher's Books. You can ask your learners to carry out both *writing tasks* in the Writing tool in the Online Workbook for homework. Then you can mark their written work and feed back to your learners online.

- a gradebook which allows you to track your learners' progress throughout the course. This can help structure a one-to-one review with the learner or be used as a record of learning. You can also use this to help you decide what to review in class.

- games for vocabulary and language practice which are not scored in the gradebook.

The Cambridge LMS provides the following tools:

- Blogs

The class blog can be used for free writing practice to consolidate learning and share ideas. For example, you could ask each learner to post a description of their holiday (or another event linked to a topic covered in class). You could ask them to read and comment on two other learners' posts.

- Forums

The forums can be used for discussions. You could post a discussion question (taken from the next lesson) and encourage learners to post their thoughts on the question for homework.

- Wikis

In each class there is a Wiki. You can set up pages within this. The wikis are ideal for whole class project work. You can use the wiki to practice process writing and to train the students to redraft and proof-read. Try not to correct students online. Take note of common errors and use these to create a fun activity to review the language in class. See www.cambridge.org/unlock for more ideas on using these tools with your class.

How to access the Cambridge LMS and setup classes

Go to **www.cambridge.org/unlock** for more information for teachers on accessing and using the Cambridge LMS and Online Workbooks.

---

8 Using *Unlock* interactive eBooks

Unlock Reading & Writing Skills Student's Books are available as fully interactive eBooks. The content of the printed Student's book and the Student's eBook is the same. However, there will be a number of differences in the way some content appears.

If you are using the interactive eBooks on tablet devices in the classroom, you may want to

consider how this affects your class structure. For example, your learners will be able to independently access the video and audio content via the eBook. This means learners could do video activities at home and class time could be optimised on discussion activities and other productive tasks. Learners can compare their responses to the answer key in their eBooks which means the teacher may need to spend less time on checking answers with the whole class, leaving more time to monitor learner progress and help individual learners.

9 Using mobile technology in the language learning classroom

By Michael Pazinas, Curriculum and assessment coordinator for the Foundation Program at the United Arab Emirates University.

The presiding learning paradigm for mobile technology in the language classroom should be to create as many meaningful learning opportunities as possible for its users. What should be at the core of this thinking is that while modern mobile technology can be a 21st century 'super-toolbox', it should be there to support a larger learning strategy. Physical and virtual learning spaces, content and pedagogy all need to be factored in before deciding on delivery and ultimately the technological tools needed.

It is with these factors in mind, that the research projects featured in this Teacher's Book aim to add elements of hands-on inquiry, collaboration, critical thinking and analysis. They have real challenges, which learners have to research and find solutions for. In an ideal world, they can become tangible, important solutions. While they are designed with groups in mind, there is nothing to stop them being used with individuals. They can be fully enriching experiences, used as starting points or simply ideas to be adapted and streamlined. When used in these ways, learner devices can become research libraries, film, art and music studios, podcast stations, marketing offices and blog creation tools.

Michael has first-hand experience of developing materials for the paperless classroom. He is the author of the Research projects which feature in the Teacher's Books.

GLOBALIZATION

Learning objectives

Focus learners on the Learning objectives box and tell them that this is what they will be working on in this unit. Later they will write an essay: 'How have eating habits changed in your country? Suggest some reasons why.' Show learners this essay title on page 29 but reassure them that all the work in this unit will help them to write it. At the end of the unit they will be able to assess how well they can manage the skills in the Learning objectives box.

UNLOCK YOUR KNOWLEDGE

Lead-in

Give learners one minute to think of as much food as possible that they have eaten in the last 24 hours. They note this down. Give them a few minutes for to check vocabulary and spelling in a dictionary. Tell them that they are going to spell the names of some food in English. Everybody starts with three points. One person says the first letter of a food on their list and the next person says another letter that together with the first makes the beginning of a food word. The next learner adds another letter and so on. If at any time someone doubts that the learner who says a letter has a real (correctly spelled) food word in mind, they can challenge that person. If the challenged learner can't give an appropriate answer, they lose a point and a new word is started. If they can give a word, the challenger loses a point. If somebody can't continue a word, they also lose a point. The winner is the last learner with points remaining at the end of the game.

👥 👥👥 Learners read the questions. To check vocabulary with weaker groups you could ask the following questions:

- Which two words in the questions mean 'things'? (items and goods)
- Which verb means to buy goods from other countries to sell in this country? (import)
- What is the opposite of the verb 'import'? (export)
- What are the nouns for goods that are imported and exported? (imports/exports)
- Which word from the questions refers to how things spread around the world? (globalization /ˌɡləʊ.bəl.aɪˈzeɪ.ʃən/)

Allow learners a few minutes to think about their answers to the questions. Then they discuss the questions in pairs. Monitor to help with vocabulary and to check their level of existing knowledge. If they are struggling, you could give

some prompts (see answers below). Check a few answers with the class. Encourage learners to react to each other's ideas.

Possible answers

2 Some people argue that importing goods gives people the opportunity to buy a wider range of goods at lower prices. Others argue that it can harm local manufacturing businesses when cheaper imports come into the country.
3 Globalization may have had effects in areas such as: food, culture, media, language, business and education.

WATCH AND LISTEN

Video script

A WORLD OF FOOD IN ONE CITY

New York, from melting pot to cooking pot.

As international trade routes, migration, media and IT communication expand across traditional borders, different cultures interact more, with a flow of goods, labour and ideas. This is called globalization.

Although this is common all over the world, there are certain cities where this is more obvious than others. New York is perhaps the best example of a city where different cultures have come together through globalization. A centre for migration for many centuries, New York is home to many ethnic groups, often living in the same neighbourhoods.

This can be clearly seen by the huge variety of world food on sale. Immigrants from Central Europe, South America, Italy, the Caribbean and China have brought their food with them. New York often took these recipes and gave them a twist to create a new American identity such as ice cream sundaes, burgers and hot dogs.

There are over 19 thousand restaurants in New York and every type of international food is represented, South American, Irish, Middle Eastern and Indian. In Harlem there are famous restaurants serving Afro-American food with chicken and rice dishes. Some have even developed into brands selling prepared food in supermarkets and recipe books.

New York has always been called a 'melting pot' as different communities have come together in one city. This means that all different ingredients, recipe books and cooking equipment are available in the shops and markets.

PREPARING TO WATCH

UNDERSTANDING KEY VOCABULARY

1 👤👥 Learners read all the sentences and complete them with the words or phrases from the box. Allow them to use dictionaries if necessary. Learners compare answers. Check answers with the class.

> ### Answers
>
> 1 labour 2 international media 3 IT communication
> 4 ethnic /ˈeθ.nɪk/ groups 5 South American
> 6 prepared food 7 cooking equipment
> 8 international cuisine

> ### Optional activity
>
> Focus learners on the word *migration* /maɪˈɡreɪ.ʃən/ and establish that it means people moving to live in different countries. Elicit the related verb *migrate* and the noun for a person (*migrant*). Also elicit verb *emigrate* (leaving a country to live in another), *emigration* (noun) and noun for a person (*emigrant*) and nouns *immigration* and *immigrant* (coming to a new country to live; a person). Relate the prefixes *em-* and *im-* to the words *export* and *import* raised in the Lead-in section.

USING YOUR KNOWLEDGE TO PREDICT CONTENT

2 👥 Tell learners they are going to watch a video about food in New York. Learners discuss the questions. Monitor to help with vocabulary and ask the class for some of their predictions. Do not give answers at this stage.

3 ▶ Learners watch the video to check their ideas. They compare answers. Check answers with the class.

> ### Possible answers
>
> 1 It is a city in the USA, sometimes called the Big Apple. Many people from different countries have moved to live there, so the culture is very international.
> 2 Hamburgers, hot dogs, fried chicken, fries, cola drinks, pizza, tacos etc.
> 3 Because New York is a very large city with a mixed, multicultural population and mixed culinary traditions, it has many types of restaurants.

WHILE WATCHING

UNDERSTANDING DETAIL

4 ▶👤👥 Before watching the video again, focus learners on the notes. They read the notes and predict the missing words or types of words. They compare answers and watch the video to check and write one word in each gap. Learners compare answers. Check answers with the class. Display the correct words.

> ### Answers
>
> 1 media 2 traditional 3 labour 4 obvious 5 cultures
> 6 migration 7 ethnic 8 variety 9 identity

WORKING OUT FROM CONTEXT

5 👤👥 Focus learners on the four multiple-choice questions. Tell them that they should try and work out the meaning of the words or phrases in italics from what they have learned from the video. Do the first question together with the class. If learners find this difficult, play the video again. Learners compare answers. Check answers with the class.

> ### Answers
>
> 1 a 2 d 3 d 4 c

DISCUSSION

6 👥👥👥 Focus learners on the questions. The answers should be based on learners' knowledge, they are not given in the video. Learners discuss their ideas. Check some answers with the class.

> ### Possible answers
>
> 1 America had a very open immigration policy, particularly in the 19th and early 20th century.
> 2 Since America has such global financial and cultural influence, its food companies have been able to open outlets in many countries around the world and change the way other countries eat. American-style food has been blamed for increased obesity in some countries.
> 3 This depends on the country the learners are from.

READING 1

PREPARING TO READ

USING YOUR KNOWLEDGE TO PREDICT CONTENT

1 Tell learners that they will be doing some work to improve their reading strategies. This means they will not be using dictionaries, although it would be a good idea for them to check unknown words in a dictionary and record them *after* the class. Ask what learners know about *blogs* (you find them online; usually written by one person; sometimes (but not always) a kind of diary; usually the most recent post is at the top; other people can comment; etc.). Ask if anyone in the class writes a blog or regularly reads one.

Paraphrase or ask learners to read the information in the box. Check the meaning of *source* (where the text comes from). Focus learners on the four questions and ask them to discuss which are likely to be true about a blog post.

2 👤👥 Learners read the blog to check their predictions. They compare answers. Check answers with the class, asking for examples.

> **Answers**
> 1 T 2 F (It is unlikely that a blog would be appropriate for an academic essay; any information found would need to be checked with a reliable source.) 3 T 4 T (Unless it is an old blog post.)

UNDERSTANDING KEY VOCABULARY

3 👤👥 Learners match the words with the definitions. Monitor to check they can manage the task. If necessary, refer them to the text so they can use the context to help them. Learners compare answers in pairs. Check answers with the class.

> **Answers**
> 1 h 2 d 3 e 4 a 5 f 6 g 7 c 8 b

WHILE READING

READING FOR DETAIL

4 👤👥 Learners read the questions and read the text again to answer them. They compare answers. Check answers with the class.

> **Answers**
> 1 The food is tasty (*yummy*) and ingredients are fresh and authentic.
> 2 The food is locally sourced (it comes from the surrounding area).
> 3 Why the price of food has increased so much recently.
> 4 The fact that food prices have gone up recently due to the bad weather, and may go up more.

5 👤👥 Learners read the statements and say whether the information is true, false or if it does not say. If learners are not familiar with this type of exercise, make sure they know the difference between *false* (the text specifically gives information that shows the statement is not true) and *does not say* (the information is not mentioned in the text so it may or may not be true). You can then point out that 1 is false (F) because the text says that food is grown in an urban area, but 3 is does not say (DNS) because the writer does not say if these types of restaurants will become more common in the future. Learners continue the exercise writing *T*, *F* or *DNS* next to each one if they think they can remember. Then they read the text again to confirm. Learners compare answers. Check answers with the class.

> **Answers**
> 1 F (The food sold at Chez Fitz is grown around the London area.) 2 F (It is normally £40 and this week £55 which is a 22% increase.) 3 DNS 4 T (All food is sourced locally.) 5 DNS 6 T (It is quite expensive.)

6 👤👥 Learners scan the text to find and highlight the informal words in the exercise. To do this they just run their eyes over the text, looking for the words they need. Point out that scanning is a useful academic reading skill as it is often necessary to find specific information quickly in a text. When they have found the words they match them with formal equivalents, using the context to help them. Learners compare answers. Check answers with the class.

> **Answers**
> 1 f 2 d 3 a 4 b 5 c 6 e

READING BETWEEN THE LINES

MAKING INFERENCES FROM THE TEXT

7 👥 Focus learners on the three questions. Point out or elicit that when we 'infer' or 'make inferences', the answer is not written directly in the text and learners have to guess the answer using other information to help them. Learners discuss the questions in pairs.

> **Possible answers**
>
> 1 The blogger sounds quite negative about perfectionists: He refers to the owner of Moda as a perfectionist, but then says *but it was so delicious*. The use of *but* implies he was surprised by the fact the food was so good.
> 2 Possibly to encourage the blogger to write a positive review of Moda, which could make readers try the restaurant.
> 3 Food prices may have risen because of economic or political circumstances, weather conditions, the price of oil for transportation, etc. Or maybe the blogger bought more or different goods that were more expensive.

DISCUSSION

8 👥 👥👥 Learners discuss the questions in pairs or small groups. Give them a few minutes to think about their opinions and language they may need to express them before they start speaking. Monitor to help with vocabulary and to encourage participation. Check a few answers with the class. Encourage learners to respond to each other's ideas.

> **Answers will vary.**

READING 2

> **Optional lead-in (1)**
>
> Ask learners if they like Italian food. Why do they think it is so popular worldwide? Elicit some Italian dishes and any restaurants where it is served in the town where the class is studying.

PREPARING TO READ

PREDICTING CONTENT FROM TOPIC SENTENCES

1 👤👥 Paraphrase or ask learners to read the information in the box. Ask learners why texts are broken into paragraphs (to make them

easier to read) and what the writer should include in each paragraph (information or opinions about the same topic). Focus learners on the five sentences. Say that they are the topic sentences of the five paragraphs in an essay. Elicit what kind of information they expect to find in Paragraph 1. Learners discuss the other topic sentences in pairs. Elicit a few answers from the class, but do not say if they are right or wrong.

2 👤👥 Learners skim read the text to check their predictions. Remind them that they do not need to focus on each word in the text, just get the gist of it. Learners compare answers. Check answers with the class.

> **Answers**
>
> 1 Italian restaurants are very popular worldwide. Italian eating habits have also changed.
> 2 Until recently, most food was homemade and only local food was available.
> 3 Italians eat more frozen foods, takeaway meals, dried pasta, ready-made pasta sauces and foreign food.
> 4 Advantages: greater range of food available and less time needed to cook it. Disadvantages: Local and national cuisine dying out.
> 5 There is more choice but it might be damaging traditions. However, it is likely that the popularity of Italian food means it will survive.

WHILE READING

READING FOR MAIN IDEAS

3 👤 Learners read the question and the table.

Draw attention to the example answer, asking learners how we know it refers to the present ('now' and the use of present tense). Learners complete the table. They compare answers. Check answers with the class.

> **Answers**
>
> 1 Present 1, 5, 6, 7 Past 2, 3 Both 4

4 👤👥 Focus learners on the four sentence beginnings. Ask them how they could complete the first sentence. Learners work alone to complete the sentences by referring to the text. They compare answers. Check answers with the class.

> **Possible answers**
>
> 1 all over the world
> 2 much more at home
> 3 convenience foods and foreign foods
> 4 is eaten less regularly

READING BETWEEN THE LINES

IDENTIFYING PURPOSE AND AUDIENCE

> **Optional lead-in (2)**
>
> Tell learners about some things you have read in the last 24 hours. Tell them who you think the texts were written for and what the author's main intention was. They then discuss what they have read, who the text was meant to appeal to and what they think the author's main intention was.

5 👤👥 Learners answer the two multiple-choice questions about the essay on Italian food. They compare answers. Check answers with the class.

> **Answers**
>
> 1 a 2 c

DISCUSSION

6 👥👥👥 Allow learners a few minutes to read the questions and think about their answers. They discuss the questions in pairs or small groups. Monitor to help with vocabulary and to encourage participation. Check a few answers with the class. Encourage learners to react to each other's ideas.

> **Answers will vary.**

⊙ LANGUAGE DEVELOPMENT

ACADEMIC ALTERNATIVES TO PHRASAL VERBS

1 👤👥 Paraphrase or ask learners to read the information in the box. Ask for some more examples of phrasal verbs. Learners match the phrasal verbs with the academic verbs. To challenge stronger learners, ask them to cover one of the columns and guess what the corresponding academic verb or phrasal verb is. Then they uncover the column and complete the exercise. Learners compare answers. Check answers with the class.

> **Answers**
>
> 1 b 2 a 3 g 4 c 5 i 6 d 7 h 8 e 9 f

2 👤 Unless they are weak, learners cover their answers to the previous exercise. Point out that they may need to change the tense of the academic verb in their answers. Do one or two with the class as examples. Learners match the words. They compare answers. Check answers with the class.

> **Answers**
>
> 1 increase 2 continue 3 studying 4 confusing
> 5 excluded 6 refused 7 exhausted 8 separate
> 9 removed

GLOBALIZATION VOCABULARY

3 👤 Learners complete the text with the words in the box, using dictionaries if necessary. Stronger ones can try completing the text without looking at the words in the box first. Remind learners to read the whole text first before they start filling in words. Learners compare answers. Check answers with the class.

> **Answers**
>
> 1 multinational 2 outlets 3 obesity 4 monopoly
> 5 poverty 6 diet 7 farms 8 supermarkets
> 9 consumption

CRITICAL THINKING

> Give learners a minute to read the Writing task they will do at the end of the unit (an essay, *How have eating habits changed in your country? Suggest some reasons why.*) and keep it in mind as they do the next exercises.

UNDERSTAND

1 👤👥 Paraphrase or ask learners to read the information in the box. Focus learners on the table and look at the first statement together. Find the supporting example in the essay in Reading 2 on page 21. (see answers below). Learners continue the task by finding the other statements in the text and writing them in the table. They can write notes rather than full sentences. Learners compare answers. Check answers with the class.

> **Answers**
>
> 1 Pasta and sauce was traditionally made at home.
> 2 Only pizza and pasta was available.
> 3 Frozen or takeaway Italian meals have become very popular in Italy.
> 4 Foreign food is becoming more readily available.
> 5 Italians are eating less home cooked food.

APPLY

2 👤👥 Paraphrase or ask learners to read the information in the box. Focus learners on the table. Ensure that learners understand that they are writing about their own country but using the *type* of information given in Exercise 1. Elicit one statement from the whole class and ask where that should be written. Now elicit a supporting example. Learners continue the activity. They discuss in pairs and write more information in the table. Monitor to help with language if necessary.

Learners share ideas for the essay later.

WRITING

GRAMMAR FOR WRITING

NOUN PHRASES

> #### Optional lead-in (1)
>
> Write on the board: *New York is perhaps the best example of a city where different cultures have come together through globalization*. Learners identify in the sentence:
>
> - some adjectives (*best, different*)
> - some prepositions (*of, through*)
> - a relative clause (*where different cultures have come together through globalization*)
> - some nouns (*New York, example, city, cultures, globalization*)
>
> Point out that New York is actually two words but one noun in meaning. Explain that other combinations of words which include nouns can make noun phrases. In the sentence above there are some noun phrases: *the best example of a city, a city where different cultures have come together through globalization* or even *the best example of a city where different cultures have come together through globalization*.

1 👤👥 Paraphrase or ask learners to read the information in the box. If noun phrases are new to them, try to elicit some more of each type of noun phrase based on the word *building*. Some examples are:

Other nouns: school building; government buildings; building site; building supplier

Relative clauses: the building where he lives; the building which was knocked down

Prepositional phrases: the building at the end of the street; the back of the building

Adjectives: a beautiful building; that stone building

Two nouns with *of*: a great number of buildings; a huge variety of buildings

Focus learners on the noun phrases and grammar structures. Match the first one together with the class to ensure they understand what to do. Learners compare answers. Check answers with the class.

> #### Answers
> 1 d 2 b 3 a 4 c

2 👤👥 Focus learners on the words *specialities* and *local*. Ask which is the noun (*specialities*, as adjectives are never plural) and which is the adjective (*local*). Ask why the example is the correct order (in English adjectives come before nouns). With a weak group do another one or two together as a class. Learners put the words in the right order to make noun phrases. They compare answers. Check answers with the class.

> #### Answers
> 1 local specialities
> 2 a list of traditional dishes
> 3 television cookery programmes
> 4 a noticeable increase in diabetes and allergies / allergies and diabetes
> 5 a variety of new fruits
> 6 the number of international chefs
> 7 the impact of different cultures
> 8 a great deal of time and preparation

TIME PHRASES

> #### Optional lead-in (2)
>
> To lead into the concept of time phrases, ask learners to write the name of a food they did not like when they were a child but do eat now. Ask some to make complete sentences with their answers, such as *I didn't like tomatoes when I was a child but now I eat them nearly every day*. Write the time phrases that learners use on the board. Then ask the class to say which are about the present and which are about the past.

3 👤👥 Paraphrase or ask learners to read the information in the box. Focus on the table and ask them where *historically* should be placed (*general past time* because we do not know the specific time). Learners continue writing the time phrases in the correct columns.

Learners compare answers. Check answers with the class.

Answers

general past time	specific past time	present
historically in the past in recent years formerly	around ten years ago in the 1970s before the war in the eighteenth century	currently these days nowadays at the present time presently

4 As a class, learners read the sentence beginnings. They work in small groups and discuss possible ways to complete them so they are true about their country. You could allow them to make changes to the sentence stems, for example, they may want to change the *1980s* to a different decade. Monitor to help with vocabulary. If learners are short of information or ideas, help with some ideas of your own. Point out that they will need this information for their essay later. Check answers with the class. Suggest learners make notes of others' ideas to help them with their essays.

Possible answers

1 ... food from all over the world.
2 ... Thai, Japanese and Lebanese.
3 ... many of the international foods we can buy now in supermarkets.
4 ... ways to save time in the kitchen.
5 ... as much Polish food as you can now in the UK.
6 ... locally-grown food.
7 ... a good range of food in small towns and villages.

ACADEMIC WRITING SKILLS

ESSAY TYPES

1 Ask learners whether they think an academic essay should give only reasons to support one opinion or whether it should be a balanced description of different opinions on the subject. (It depends on the essay question. Both are possible and there are also other essay types). Learners read the information in the box and the four essay titles and decide which type of essay from the box each one represents. They compare answers. Check answers with the class.

Answers

1 Defending an argument 2 Problem – Solution
3 For and against 4 Cause and effect

ESSAY STRUCTURE

2 Learners read the information in the box and the five extracts and decide whether each one comes from the introduction, a body paragraph or the conclusion of an essay. They compare answers. Check answers with the class. If learners have different answers from the ones given here, accept them if they can justify them well.

Suggested answers

1 conclusion 2 introduction 3 a body paragraph
4 a body paragraph 5 a body paragraph.

WRITING TASK

Focus learners on the writing task. Check they understand the title fully by asking the following questions:

- Which essay type is it? (Cause and effect.)
- What eating habits could it include? (Meal times, frequency of eating out, eating at the table or in front of the TV, increase in foreign foods available, eating between meals, food shopping, etc.)
- What time period should it refer to? (Past and present.)
- Is it better to write about one change and then one reason why, another change and the reason why, etc., or to write about several changes and then reasons why these have all happened? (Both styles are acceptable, but it is important to be consistent.)

Learners discuss ideas for the essay in pairs. They talk about the changes and some possible reasons. Refer them back to their work in the Critical thinking and Grammar for writing sections if they are having trouble. Monitor to help with language and prompt with ideas if necessary.

PLAN AND WRITE A FIRST DRAFT

1 Check that learners understand what a first draft is (a first attempt at writing that will probably change, and not the final essay). Focus learners on the exercise and Reading text 2 on Page 21. They match each paragraph in the text with one of the functions in the exercise.

Learners compare answers in pairs. Check answers with the class.

Answers

a 3 b 1 c 5 d 4 e 2

2 ▲ Learners now write the function of each of their five paragraphs in column A. They do not need to use the same structure as the essay in Reading 2. Monitor to check that the organization is logical.

3 ▲ Learners now make notes about what they will write in each paragraph in column B, keeping its function in mind. Give learners the opportunity to ask you questions about vocabulary and spellings of new words or use dictionaries. Tell them they will not be allowed to use dictionaries while they are writing.

4 ▲ Learners write the first draft of their essay following their plans. Allow about 40 minutes for this. They should write at least 250 words and highlight any language (including spelling) of which they are unsure. Give them a warning five minutes before the end of the set time.

EDIT

5–8 ▲ To encourage learners to take responsibility for their own learning, tell them to check their writing using the task checklist. Stress that this is a very important part of the writing process as it helps learners to learn from their mistakes. Encourage them to look back over their plan and at the unit.

OBJECTIVES REVIEW

See Introduction, page 9 for ideas about using the Objectives review with your learners.

WORDLIST

See Introduction, page 9 for ideas about how to make the most of the Wordlist with your learners.

REVIEW TEST

See page 95 for the photocopiable Review test for this unit and page 92 for ideas about when and how to administer the Review test.

MODEL ANSWER

See page 125 for the photocopiable Model answer.

RESEARCH PROJECT

Investigate and give a presentation on how globalization has affected your country.

Divide the class into groups and ask them to think about globalization and their own country. They should research the following points: the effect of the internet, culture, food and international businesses on their country. They can also think about the migration of people and the advantages and disadvantages for the local economy.

These points should be divided between the groups so that each one can investigate a different theme comparing changes between now and the past. Each group should then present their findings to the class.

EDUCATION

Learning objectives

Focus learners on the Learning objectives box and tell them that this is what they will be working on in this unit. Later they will write an essay: '*Outline the various differences between studying a language and studying mathematics. In what ways may they in fact be similar?*' Show learners this essay title on page 48 but reassure them that all the work in this unit will help them to write it. At the end of the unit they will be able to assess how well they can manage the skills in the Learning objectives box.

UNLOCK YOUR KNOWLEDGE

Lead-in

Show learners the following simile (or use a different one of your own if you prefer):

A good lesson is like a meal because it satisfies you and gives you the fuel to live your life.

Check learners understand that in this sentence 'meal' is a simile /ˈsɪm.ɪ.li/ because we are comparing it to a good lesson using the structure ___ *is like* ___. Now replace the sentence with:

A good education is like _____ *because* _____.

Ask if learners can think of a simile to complete the sentence. If they cannot, give these prompts: light, food, a key, a ship, a tree, money and ask them to complete the sentence. Learners share their ideas with the class, justifying their similes.

👥 👥👥 Learners read the questions. Check that they are aware that 'state education' in the UK (called 'public education' in the US) is provided by the government. Higher or further education may not necessarily be free. In the UK, 'public school' means a type of private or independent school that is usually very expensive. If your learners are all from the same country, they can imagine they have to explain their education system to somebody from another country for Question 1. Learners discuss the questions in pairs or small groups. Monitor to help with vocabulary and to check their level of existing knowledge. Check a few answers with the class. Encourage learners to react to each other's ideas.

| Answers will vary.

WATCH AND LISTEN

Video script

BECOMING A GONDOLIER

Narrator: Gondolas are a traditional form of transport along the canals of Venice in Italy. The people who steer the boats are called gondoliers. They play an important role in Venetian life and so they have a high status in the city. Being a gondolier is a prestigious and well-paid job. Gondolas are privately owned and the profession usually passes from father to son.

There are just 425 members of the profession in the whole city, and it is very rare for a woman to be a gondolier.

Becoming a gondolier takes years of practice because it is a very skilled job. Apprentice gondoliers have to take an exam before they can join the profession. Passing the exam is incredibly difficult and only three people pass each year. Alessandro has been an apprentice for three years. Unusually, he is the first in his family to train to be a gondolier. He has had an experienced gondolier teaching him.

Alessandro: It's my dream to be a gondolier. It will make me very proud.

Narrator: It is the day of the exam. Alessandro is nervous. If he passes the exam, his family will be able to stay in Venice. If he fails, they will have to move out of Venice and find work elsewhere. The examiners watch his skills carefully. He must show how well he can steer the boat. The canals are very narrow, and Alessandro must be careful not to touch the sides, or he will lose marks. Other obstacles are low bridges and building work. It is the moment of truth, and Alessandro will find out if he has passed his exam or not.

Examiner: We've discussed your exam result, and we're pleased to let you know that you're a gondolier! Well done!

Narrator: The three years of hard training have paid off. Alessandro is now a fully qualified gondolier, and proudly wears the distinctive uniform of stripy shirt and straw hat. He can now provide for his family and settle down in Venice, his hometown.

PREPARING TO WATCH

USING YOUR KNOWLEDGE

1 👥 Learners discuss the three questions. If you think they will know very little about Venice, refer them to the pictures. Check answers with the class.

Answers

1 Italy
2 Many tourists visit Venice to see the famous canals and ride in a gondola.
3 There are many jobs which serve the tourist industry in Venice, such as shopkeepers, waiters and gondoliers.

UNDERSTANDING KEY VOCABULARY

2 👤👥 Focus learners on the three words in the example. Establish that two of them have very similar meanings, while the other (*easy*) has a very different meaning. With a weak group, do another example together and encourage dictionary use. Learners circle the word in each set that has a different meaning. They compare answers in pairs. Check answers with the class, asking learners to justify their answers.

Answers

1 easy 2 ticket 3 discussion 4 apprentice /ə'pren.tɪs/
5 hobby 6 general

3 👤👥 Learners complete the sentences with the two similar words (not the ones they have circled). The order in which they write the words is not important. They compare answers. Check answers with the class.

Answers

1 qualified, experienced (*qualified* means you have certificates, diplomas, etc., *experienced* means you have been doing the job for a long time)
2 difficult, challenging /'tʃæl.ɪn.dʒɪŋ/ (although both mean the opposite of *easy*, *challenging* sounds more positive than *difficult*)
3 licence /'laɪ.səns/, permit (a *licence* is usually long-term or permanent, whereas a *permit* is usually for a limited time)
4 distinctive, original (*distinctive* means you can easily see how something is different from others, *original* can mean that it is the only one like that)
5 exam, test (an *exam* – short for *examination* – is usually more formal than a *test*)
6 job, profession (a *job* is the work you are paid for, a *profession* is a type of work which needs a high level of training or skill, such as a doctor. A learner of law may take a holiday job as a tour guide, for example, but hope to work in the legal profession.)

WHILE WATCHING

LISTENING FOR KEY INFORMATION

4 👥 Tell learners they are going to watch a video about gondoliers [ˌgɒn.də'lɪərz]. Learners look at the statements and predict whether they are true or false. Ask the class for some of their predictions. Do not give answers at this stage.

5 ▶️👥 Learners watch the video to check their answers. They compare answers. Check answers with the class.

Answers

1 F (it is rare for a gondolier to be female.) 2 T 3 F (They have been around for many years.) 4 T 5 T 6 F (They wear a uniform of a stripy shirt and hat.)

UNDERSTANDING DETAIL

6 ▶️👤👥 Before watching the video again, learners read the notes and see if they can spot any mistakes in the information (not language). They watch the video to check and correct any mistakes in the notes that they find. Learners compare answers in pairs. Check answers with the class.

Answers

1 Wrong (Candidates study on the job as apprentices, not at university.) 2 Wrong (Candidates are marked down if they touch the sides of the canal or a bridge.) 3 Wrong (Candidates should be careful if there are low bridges.) 4 Wrong (Only 3 licences are awarded annually.) 5 Correct 6 Wrong (They wear stripy shirts.)

RESPONDING TO THE VIDEO CONTENT

7 ▶️👤👥 Learners try to remember four reasons why Venetians want to become gondoliers. They write these down and compare answers with a partner. Then they watch the video again to check.

Possible answers

1 Gondoliers play an important role in Venetian life.
2 Gondoliers have a high status in the city / a prestigious job.
3 Being a gondolier is a well paid job.
4 Gondoliers live and work in Venice.

8 👥 Focus learners on the question. Make sure learners understand that in English *career* means your profession, but not your training or education. They discuss the question related to their own dream career or studies. Check some answers with the class.

DISCUSSION

9 👥👥👥 Focus learners on the questions. The answers should be based on learners' own knowledge as they are not given in the video. Give learners a short time to think about their answers before they start speaking. They discuss their ideas. Monitor to encourage participation and help with unknown language. Check some answers with the class.

> **Answers**
> Answers will vary.

READING 1

PREPARING TO READ

UNDERSTANDING KEY VOCABULARY

1 👤👥 Focus learners on the table. Help them understand what is needed in each box:

- *elements of a university course* means the parts or components of it. In a school, for example, you might have lessons and terms.
- *ways to deliver education* refers to whether learners learn in classrooms or via the Internet.
- For *types of course* refer learners to the two pictures.

  Learners put the words in the box into the correct columns, using dictionaries if necessary. They compare answers. Check answers with the class.

> **Answers**
> elements of a university course: lecture, seminar, module, tutorial
> ways to deliver education: face-to-face, distance learning
> types of course: academic course, vocational /vəʊˈkeɪ.ʃən.əl/ course
> ways to pay for education: tuition /tjuːˈɪʃ.ən/ fees, scholarship

VOCABULARY IN CONTEXT

2 👤👥 Learners use the words from the previous exercise to complete the sentences. Do one or two examples together first. Learners compare answers. Check answers with the class.

> **Answers**
> 1 scholarship 2 Face-to-face 3 module 4 vocational course 5 Academic courses 6 lecture 7 Tuition fees 8 seminar 9 distance learning 10 tutorial

3 👥 Learners read the questions. Give them some time to think about their answers and check unknown vocabulary with you or in a dictionary. If your learners are from different countries or regions, ensure they are in mixed groups to discuss these questions. If they are from the same place, ask them to decide together how they would explain the answers to a foreigner.

> **Answers**
> Learner's own answers

4 👤👥 Focus learners on the web page. With weaker groups, ask them to find the part of the text that:

- tells you the name of the university (Title)
- lists some courses (Our most popular courses)
- talks about money (Frequently Asked Questions: What do they cost?)
- gives an example of a degree course (Sample course overview: BA in English Language and Literature)
- gives an example of a vocational course (Sample course overview: Diploma in teaching)

Learners answer the questions in Exercise 3 about Middletown University. Warn them that they may not be able to fully answer each question. Learners compare answers. Check answers with the class.

> **Answers**
> 1 Mathematics, English Literature and History.
> 2 Engineering, Nursing, Accounting, Plumbing, Teaching and Catering.
> 3 It does not say explicitly, but scholarships and bursaries are available for certain courses.
> 4 The English Literature and Language course is three years.
> 5 With essays, exams, dissertations and observations.

WHILE READING

5 👤👥 Focus learners on the statements and remind them of the difference between *false* and *does not say* (See Unit 1 notes, page 14). Do one or two statements with the whole class, eliciting the reasons for the answers given in the text. Check that learners understand that *pass an examination* (Question 6) means to succeed in it, not just to take it. Learners complete the exercise. They compare answers, saying what is wrong with the false statements. Check answers with the class.

Answers

1 F (Distance learning courses are also available.)
2 F (The costs vary considerably.) 3 DNS 4 T 5 DNS
6 T 7 T (You will *also* begin teaching.) 8 F (Three are compulsory.) 9 T

READING BETWEEN THE LINES

MAKING INFERENCES FROM THE TEXT

6 👥 Paraphrase the information in the box or ask learners to read it. Focus learners on Question 1 and ask them to guess the answer from the webpage. Ask some learners to explain their guesses. Sometimes they will be able to find clues in the text and sometimes they have to use their own ideas and knowledge. Learners discuss Questions 2–4. Check answers with the class.

Possible answers

1 Some courses are more expensive to run. Courses in higher demand can also charge higher fees.
2 There are fewer learners who are interested in science and education in the UK, so it is in the government's interest to promote them.
3 An aspect of literature (for example, works by a particular author or a style of literature) or language (for example, use of a particular language feature).
4 The core modules are key to understanding the background to a subject, whereas the optional modules allow deeper study into learners' particular areas of interest.
5 Because the course is practical the most useful assessment is how well learners do the job itself.

DISCUSSION

7 👥👥 Learners discuss the questions in pairs or small groups. Give them a few minutes to think about their opinions and language they may need to express them before they start speaking. Monitor to help with vocabulary and to encourage participation. Check a few answers with the class. Encourage learners to respond to each other's ideas.

Answers will vary.

READING 2

Optional lead-in

👥👥 Ask learners to think of something they have wanted to learn recently, but not as part of their formal education; for example, how to fix something, background information about a news item, or how to use a piece of technology or software. How did they learn it? Did they use books, other people or the Internet? Learners discuss their experiences and try to identify what is best studied face-to-face and what is better learnt on-line.

PREPARING TO READ

UNDERSTANDING KEY VOCABULARY

1 👤👥👥 Focus learners on the collocations in the left-hand column. Ask if they can find another collocation in the right-hand column which has a similar meaning to *distance learning* from the text in Reading 1. They may find several possibilities but they should choose the best one (*online course*). Learners match the collocations with their meanings. They compare answers. Check answers with the class.

Answers

1 f 2 h 3 i 4 e 5 d 6 a 7 c 8 b 9 g

2 👥👥 Learners discuss what they know about distance learning by saying whether they think the statements are true or false. Emphasize that they are not expected to know the answers to the questions, just give their opinions. Do not give any answers to these questions at this stage.

3 👤👥👥 Learners read the article to check their answers, noting why the false answers are wrong. Learners compare answers. Check answers with the class.

Answers

1 F (It dates back around 200 years.) 2 F (The first virtual university began in 1996.) 3 T 4 F (The teacher may seldom or never meet their learners.) 5 T 6 F (Both systems can produce positive results.)

WHILE READING

READING FOR MAIN IDEAS

4 👤👥 Focus learners on the five paragraph descriptions and check they understand *knowledge transfer* (passing information from one person to another) and *peer* [pɪər] (people who work or study together, who usually have similar ages or levels of responsibility). Learners match the descriptions with the paragraphs in the magazine article. They compare answers. Check answers with the class.

> **Answers**
> 1 B 2 E 3 C 4 A 5 D

5 👤👥 Learners read the text again to decide which kind of learning (or both) the statements in the table refer to. The first one is given as an example. Learners compare answers. Check answers with the class.

> **Answers**
> 2 distance 3 distance 4 face-to-face 5 both
> 6 distance 7 distance 8 both

> **Optional activity**
>
> Learners look at the text again, but cover Exercise 1. Ask them to highlight any of the collocations they can find that they studied earlier. Learners compare answers, trying to find the nine different collocations. Check answers with the class. If learners are preparing to study the same academic subject, refer them to a text to highlight and record collocations in it that refer specifically to their subject. If learners are preparing to study different subjects, suggest they do this individually at home with a text of their choice.

READING BETWEEN THE LINES

MAKING INFERENCES FROM THE TEXT

6 👥 Learners discuss the questions. Point out that they need to use their own knowledge and ideas to answer them. Check answers with the class.

> **Possible answers**
>
> 1 Because they consider distance learning to be directly linked to technological advances.
> 2 Because you do not generally meet your teachers face-to-face, you communicate with them in an online forum.
> 3 They are able to discuss ideas and develop their knowledge together.
> 4 The author sees both the strengths and weaknesses of distance learning.

DISCUSSION

7 👥👥👥 Learners discuss the questions in pairs or small groups. Give them a few minutes to think about their opinions and language they may need to express them before they start speaking. Monitor to help with vocabulary and to encourage participation. Check a few answers with the class. Encourage learners to respond to each other's ideas.

> **Answers will vary.**

👁 LANGUAGE DEVELOPMENT

EDUCATION VOCABULARY

1 👤👥 Learners use dictionaries to check vocabulary where necessary and complete the sentences. *Peer-reviewed* means that a piece of writing has been evaluated by professionals in the same field of study to determine if the standard is good enough for publication. Learners compare answers. Check answers with the class.

> **Answers**
> 1 assignment 2 examination 3 term 4 semester
> 5 plagiarism 6 journal 7 dissertation 8 lecturer
> 9 tutor

ACADEMIC WORDS

2 👤👥 All the words in this exercise have already been seen in this unit. Weaker learners can refer back to previous exercises to help them. Dictionaries could also be used. Learners match words with their meanings. They compare answers. Check answers with the class.

> **Answers**
> 1 d 2 a 3 f 4 h 5 i 6 k 7 j 8 g 9 c 10 b 11 e

3 👤👥 Learners work alone to complete the sentences with some of the academic words from the previous exercise. They compare answers. Check answers with the class.

> **Answers**
> 1 alternative 2 interaction 3 aspects 4 principles
> 5 motivation 6 specific 7 core 8 virtual

CRITICAL THINKING

Give learners a minute to read the Writing task they will do at the end of the unit (an essay, *Outline the various differences between studying a language and studying mathematics. In what ways may they in fact be similar?*) and keep it in mind as they do the next exercises.

ANALYZE

1 Focus learners on the Venn diagram and ask them the following questions:

- What is this type of visual organizer called? (a Venn diagram [ˌvenˈdaɪ.ə.grœm])
- What is it used for? (Organizing items by category and seeing where they have something in common.)
- How are they used? (Items are written in the appropriate circles, and items that fall into both categories are written in the overlapping part.)

Learners decide where the words in the box should be on the Venn diagram, using dictionaries if necessary.

Learners compare answers. Check answers with the class. You could do this by displaying a large Venn diagram at the front of the class and asking learners to come up and write the answers in it. Learners justify their choices or objections. There are no right or wrong answers as different courses for the same subject may vary.

Possible answers

Academic: Philosophy; Art history; Mathematics; Biochemistry
Vocational: Hairdressing; Beauty therapy; Golf course management; Catering; Construction
Both: Law; Business administration; Medicine; Electrical engineering; Computer science

2 Working in small groups, learners add more subjects that they can think of to the Venn diagram. They can use dictionaries to check spelling. Refer them back to Reading 1 for more ideas. Check answers with the class. Write their ideas in the displayed Venn diagram (see above).

3 Focus learners on the opinions about whether it is better to study a vocational course or an academic course. Do the first opinion together. Warn them that there may be some language they do not understand,

but they only need to recognize the speaker's viewpoint. Learners read the opinions and compare answers. Check answers with the class.

Answers

1 academic 2 vocational 3 vocational 4 academic
5 vocational 6 academic

4 Allow learners time to read the questions and think about their answers. They discuss the questions. Monitor to help with vocabulary and to encourage participation. Open the discussion up to the whole class. Check a few answers with the class. Encourage learners to react to each other's ideas.

WRITING

GRAMMAR FOR WRITING

COMPARISON AND CONTRAST LANGUAGE

Optional lead-in

To revise vocabulary and lead into the idea of comparison and contrast, this speaking activity revises language from earlier in the unit. Learners close their books. Display the following:

What are the similarities and differences between:

1... an examination, assignment and a dissertation?

2... a term and a semester?

3... a tutor and a lecturer?

4... a journal and an ordinary magazine?

5... plagiarism and quoting from other writers?

Note that the verb *quote* /kwəʊt/ means to repeat or reference someone else's words. Learners discuss the differences. Monitor to help with unknown language. Check answers with the class.

Answers

1 They are all pieces of academic writing. An *examination* is written under timed, controlled conditions, an *assignment* is a normal piece of writing homework and a *dissertation* is much longer.
2 They are both parts of the academic year. If an academic year is divided into three periods we call these *terms*; if it is divided into two they are *semesters*.
3 They are both academic jobs at a university. A *lecturer* talks to a large group of people while the *tutor* works with individuals but in fact it could be the same person with different roles.

4 They both contain articles. A *journal* is academic – and it is peer-reviewed, which means articles are only accepted if experts in the field agree it is of a high enough quality. A *magazine* could be very general or about a specific subject. It often contains advertising.

5 They both use somebody else's words. *Plagiarism* is copying somebody else's work without acknowledging that it is theirs, not yours. *Quoting* is using another person's words but giving a reference to who originally said it.

1 👤👥 Either paraphrase the information in the box or ask learners to read it. Focus learners on the expression in Exercise 1. Learners discuss which phrases introduce a comparison and which introduce a contrast. Check answers with the class. Learners record these as a group of expressions which they can add to when they learn more.

| Answer Key

Comparison: In the same way; Likewise
Contrast: In contrast; Conversely

2 👤👥 Focus learners on the first sentence. Elicit the kind of information that could complete it for example something about vocational courses not leading to high-flying careers. However, point out that we need to use different language to express this so it does not sound too repetitive. Build up a sentence together on the board (see key for an example).

Learners complete the other sentences with their own ideas. Weaker learners may need to work in pairs. Monitor closely, being ready to help with synonyms. Learners compare answers, helping each other to improve their sentences. Check answers with the class.

| Possible answers

1 ...vocational courses may result in lower-paid jobs.
2 ...teaching courses require learners to both understand theory and to perform practical tasks.
3 ...vocational courses are much more practical.
4 ...fees for academic courses are not cheap.

COMPARISON AND CONTRAST LANGUAGE IN TOPIC SENTENCES

3 👤👥 Paraphrase the information in the box or ask learners to read it. Point out how we use commas when we add extra information of contrast or comparison in topic sentences. Learners match the beginnings and endings of the sentences. They compare answers. Check

answers with the class. Suggest learners make notes of useful language to use in their essays.

| Answers

1 d 2 a 3 e 4 f 5 c 6 b

ACADEMIC WRITING SKILLS

ANALYZING AN ESSAY QUESTION

1 👤 Either paraphrase the information in the box or ask learners to read it. Learners read both essay titles. Make sure they know that they are the same question written in different ways.

2 👤👥 Learners write the words from essay title B that have the same meaning as the phrases from A. They compare answers. Check answers with the class.

| Answers

1 describe the (similarities and) differences (between)
2 academic study
3 vocational training
4 describe the similarities (and differences) (between)

WRITING AN INTRODUCTION TO AN ESSAY (1)

3 👤👥 Either paraphrase the information in the box or ask learners to read it. Point out that introductions do not always include all of the three features mentioned, but it is useful for learners to do this if they are new to this type of essay writing. Explain that there are six introductions to the writing task given. Learners continue the exercise, deciding which introductions follow the advice given and what is wrong with the others. They compare answers. Check answers with the class.

| Answers

1 This is not a good introduction as it only repeats the essay title.
2 This is not a good introduction as it answers a different question to the one given. The writer should outline similarities and differences, whereas this learner begins with a very strong opinion.
3 This is not a good introduction as it gives a personal viewpoint and it also uses very informal language.
4 This is a good introduction as it gives background information using language that is different from that used in the question; it refers to the aims of the essay, and also outlines the structure.

5 This is not a good introduction as it is about the economy rather than education. The language is also very repetitive.

6 This is not a good introduction as it refers almost exclusively to a personal example and does not refer to the question.

WRITING TASK

Focus learners on the writing task. Check they understand the title fully by asking the following questions:

- Do you have to write about advantages and disadvantages in the essay? (no)
- Will you compare or contrast studying a language and mathematics, or both? (both)
- How is this essay title different to the one you have been working on in the Academic writing skills section? (It is about a language and mathematics, not academic and vocational subjects.)
- Where will you find information, ideas and language structures for this essay? (Throughout this unit.)
- How will you structure the essay? (With an introduction, differences, similarities, and finishing with a conclusion.)

WRITING A FIRST DRAFT

1 Learners work in small groups. They brainstorm as many features as they can and write them in Venn diagram. Refer them back to page 43 if they cannot remember how to do this.

2 Now working alone, learners make a plan following the given structure. They write notes only, not complete sentences. They can use a dictionary or look back at the unit for help with language. Tell them that they will not be allowed to use a dictionary while they are writing.

3 Learners write the first draft of their essay following their plans. Allow about 40 minutes for this. They should write at least 250 words and highlight any language (including spelling) of which they are unsure. Give them a warning five minutes before the end of the set time.

EDIT

4–7 To encourage learners to take responsibility for their own learning, tell them to check their writing using the task checklist. Stress that this is a very important part of the writing process as it helps learners to learn from their mistakes. Encourage them to look back over their plan and at the unit.

OBJECTIVES REVIEW

See Introduction, page 9 for ideas about using the Objectives review with your learners.

WORDLIST

See Introduction, page 9 for ideas about how to make the most of the Wordlist with your learners.

REVIEW TEST

See page 98 for the photocopiable Review test for this unit and page 92 for ideas about when and how to administer the Review test.

MODEL ANSWER

See page 126 for the photocopiable Model answer.

RESEARCH PROJECT

Design a test to assess your knowledge of English from this unit.

Divide the class into groups. Explain that the learners will need to identify the language and skills that they most need to test from the unit. Point out the different question types available to test vocabulary like; multiple choice, matching, ordering tasks, short answer questions, fill-in-the-blank tasks, sentence writing, and extended writing. Ask them to think of the number of questions, and write the answer key, instructions and criteria by which the exam should be marked. Learners can use paper, a word processor or an online quiz website. Each group produces an exam.

When the tests are submitted, they should be copied and distributed to the groups. Each group then takes the test and the scores are analyzed. The class then rates which test was the most effective.

3 MEDICINE

Learning objectives

Focus learners on the Learning objectives box and tell them that this is what they will be working on in this unit. Later they will write an essay: 'Avoiding preventative illness is the responsibility of individuals and their families, not governments.' Do you agree?' Show learners this essay title on page 66 but reassure them that all the work in this unit will help them to write it. At the end of the unit they will be able to assess how well they can manage the skills in the Learning objectives box.

UNLOCK YOUR KNOWLEDGE

Lead-in

👥👥👥 Mime an illness or symptom such as a headache or backache and ask learners to say what it is. Learners work in small groups. One person in the group mimes a health problem and the others have to say what it is. The person who guesses the problem correctly mimes a different problem. Give them two minutes to do as many as possible. They should keep count and cannot repeat any that have already been mimed. The person with the most correct answers in the group is the winner. Monitor to help with language.

👥👥 👥👥👥 Focus learners on the list. Ask which are illnesses and which are symptoms (any feeling of illness, or physical or mental change which is caused by a particular disease).

Allow learners a few minutes to think about their answers to the questions. They discuss them in pairs or small groups. Monitor to help with vocabulary and to check their level of existing knowledge. If they are struggling, you could give some prompts (see answers below). Check a few answers with the class. Encourage learners to react to each other's ideas.

Possible answers to Question 1

a cold: take some painkillers, have a hot lemon drink, eat raw garlic
a headache: take some painkillers, drink lots of water
a cut on your hand: bandage it and raise it up, go to hospital if it is serious
toothache: go to the dentist, take painkillers
obesity: eat less, exercise more
depression: talk to a psychiatrist, take anti-depressants
stress: work less, exercise more

Optional activity

Model and drill the pronunciation of *headache* /ˈhed.eɪk/ and *toothache* /ˈtuːθ.eɪk/. Draw attention to the spelling of *ache*. Tell learners that some words that come from Ancient Greek spell the /k/ sound with *ch*. Elicit other words with the suffix *ache* (*backache*, *stomach ache*, *earache*) and ask learners to spell them. Note that some are one word, some two. Then elicit more words with the letters *ch* pronounced as /k/, for example, *school*, *chemist*, *technical*, *mechanic*. Encourage learners to notice these words in their reading, especially related to their subjects, and keep a record of them.

WATCH AND LISTEN

Video script

ALTERNATIVE MEDICINE

Ayurveda, from India, is the oldest form of medicine on the planet. Its name means roughly 'the science of long life'. It is over 3,500 years old and people still use it today. Now in India there are over 300,000 trained Ayurveda doctors and the practice has spread to alternative health centres around the world. Most of its remedies are from plants, herbs and other natural ingredients. Using plants to treat and heal diseases is not only something that Ayurveda doctors do.

People around the world use natural products in medicine. This shaman in the Peruvian rainforest also uses the things that grow around him to treat patients, using a wide range of medicines. Here in the Serengeti in Africa, we can see how people use natural resources for the same reasons.

In fact, a huge number of treatments used in what we might call 'modern medicine' come from plants – often these are the remedies used by our ancestors. For example, aspirin, one of the most common painkillers, is based on plant extracts from the bark of willow trees. Hundreds of common medicines are plant-based.

While we can learn a lot from these ancient forms of medicine, we should always be careful. The cures have not always been tested scientifically so there is a risk that using one of these ancient remedies could have no effect – or worse, could actually be dangerous. Scientists worry that some natural medicines may contain heavy metals such as lead and mercury. Nevertheless, nature is clearly a valuable source of medicine, bringing benefits to people all over the world.

PREPARING TO WATCH

UNDERSTANDING KEY VOCABULARY

1 👤 Focus learners on the two words in Question 1. Ask if they are synonyms, words with similar meanings. (yes) Learners continue the exercise, ticking the pairs of words they think are synonyms. With a weak group, do another example together and encourage dictionary use to check words learners do not know.

2 👥 Learners compare answers, saying what the differences are between the words they did not tick. Check answers with the class.

> **Answers**
>
> 1 synonyms
> 2 Not synonyms. A *hospital* is place where conventional Western medicine is used. An *alternative health centre* uses older, traditional medicine.
> 3 Synonyms, but a *disease* is always serious, whereas an *illness* is a more general word covering all types of sickness.
> 4 Not synonyms. *Natural* means originating from nature. *Synthetic* means man-made.
> 5 synonyms

USING VISUALS TO PREDICT CONTENT

3 👥 Learners look at the photos together to predict content of the video.

> **Suggested answer**
>
> Herbal medicine.

4 👥 Learners discuss whether the statements are true. Ask the class for some of their predictions. Do not give answers at this stage.

5 ▶ 👥 Learners watch the video to check. They compare answers in pairs. Check answers with the class.

> **Answers**
>
> 1 True 2 True 3 False. Traditional remedies can be dangerous, and some Ayurvedic /aɪ.ʊəˌveɪ.dɪkˈ/ medicines contain heavy metals.

WHILE WATCHING

LISTENING FOR KEY INFORMATION

6 ▶ 👥 Tell learners they are going to watch the video again. Before this, they look at the statements about Ayurveda and predict or try to remember whether they are true or false. Learners watch the video to check their answers. They compare answers in pairs. Check answers with the class.

> **Suggested answers**
>
> 1 F 2 T 3 F (It was invented over 3.500 years ago)
> 4 T (There are over 300,000 Ayurvedic doctors in India.) 5 F (There are many different treatments around the world which use plants which are not Ayurvedic medicine) 6 T

7 👤👥 Learners think of at least one example for each thing. The examples do not necessarily need to come from the video. They compare answers in pairs. Check answers with the class.

> **Possible answers**
>
> 1 aspirin, paracetamol, ibuprofen
> 2 lead, mercury, plutonium
> 3 India, Peru, African countries
> 4 herbs, bark, plants

8 👤 Ask learners why it is difficult to take notes when listening. One reason is speed – most people cannot write at the speed of speech, so it is sometimes useful to use some symbols instead of words when taking notes. Give them the following information if appropriate:

- *cf* This is an abbreviation from the Latin word *confer* which means *bring together*.
- *e.g.* This very common abbreviation is also from Latin: *exempli gratia* meaning for the sake of example.
- *etc.* This is also from Latin, and is a short form of *et cetera*, meaning *and other things*.
- *inc.* This is sometimes written as *incl*.
- *+* In typed writing this is represented by the symbol & (called ampersand).
- *#* This symbol is used more in the US. In Britain, *no.* is often used, which is an abbreviation of the Latin *numero*.

Ask learners if they use any of these symbols in note-taking in their own language. Also point out that people often leave out pronouns, articles and auxiliary words that are not necessary for the meaning when they take notes. Learners match the note-taking symbols and abbreviations. They compare answers in pairs. Check answers with the class.

> **Answers**
>
> 1 c 2 f 3 a 4 e 5 g 6 d 7 b

9 👤👥 Learners write out the notes in full sentences. If you think this will be difficult for them you could do the example sentences below together with the class:

- *Chinese medicine, inc. acupuncture & massage, > 2,500 yrs old*
(Chinese medicine, including acupuncture and massage, is over 2,500 years old.)
- *Few clinical trials cf modern medicine*
(There have been few clinical trials compared with those for modern medicine.)
- *Acupuncture may be useful for # of symptoms e.g. depression/low back pain* (Acupuncture may be useful for a number of symptoms, such as depression or low back pain.)

Learners compare answers with a partner. Check answers with the class.

> **Possible answers**
>
> 1 Ayurveda is more than 3,500 years old and there are more than 300,000 Ayurvedic doctors.
> 2 Plants used in Ayurveda are similar to other places, for example Peru and in the Serengeti.
> 3 Some medicines include metals, such as lead or mercury.

> **Optional activity**
>
> ▶ Learners watch the video again and make notes of the most important information, trying to use the symbols where possible.

RESPONDING TO THE VIDEO CONTENT

10 ▶👥 Turn the sound down completely on the video and play it again. Learners work in pairs, imagining they are the narrators and commentating on what they see. You may need to pause the video to allow them enough time to think and speak as they do this. This exercise will help them revise the language they have learnt from the video.

DISCUSSION

11 👥👥 Learners discuss the questions in pairs or small groups. Give them a few minutes to think about their opinions and the language they may need to express them before they start speaking. Monitor to help with vocabulary and to encourage participation. Check a few answers with the class. Encourage learners to respond to each other's ideas.

> **Answers will vary.**

READING 1

PREPARING TO READ

SKIMMING FOR KEY WORDS

> **Background information**
>
> The reading text in this section refers to the NHS, the British National Health Service. This provides free or very cheap healthcare for all UK citizens and is paid for by the government through taxation. The text features a general practitioner, or GP. This is a doctor who provides general medical treatment for people who live in a particular area. In the UK, if you are ill, you visit the GP. You only go to hospital in an emergency or if your GP has made an appointment for you to see a specialist there. Tell learners that this section will help them considerably with the writing task later in the unit.

1 👤👥 Paraphrase or ask learners to read the information in the box. Point out the sub-headings (*Homeopathy should be state funded* and *Homeopathy should not be state funded*). If learners ask what homeopathy /ˌhəʊ.miˈɒp.ə.θi/ is, tell them that it is a form of alternative healthcare and that they will find out more when they read. Learners skim the title and introduction and underline the words.

2 👤👥 Learners read the title, introduction and the sub-headings of the article to decide on the main idea of the article. They compare answers in pairs, justifying their answers. Check answers with the class.

> **Answers**
>
> Number 3 best describes the main idea of the article. Number 1 is incorrect as the article is about a form of alternative medicine. Number 2 is incorrect as the article focuses on opinions on the effectiveness of homeopathy. Number 4 is incorrect as the article does not focus on a range of alternative medical treatments, just homeopathy.

3 👤👥 Learners look at the words in the box from Exercise 1 and try to match them to the definitions given. Do not allow dictionary use. Explain that this is good practice for times when they cannot use a dictionary, such as in examinations. They can use the context to help them guess as well as any clues within the words themselves. For example, they may know that *contro-* (and *contra-*) mean *against*. Learners compare answers in pairs. Check answers with the class.

> ### Answers
>
> 1 homeopathy
> 2 diluted /daɪˈluːtɪd/
> 3 fund
> 4 drugs
> 5 proponent /prəˈpəʊ.nənt/
> 6 debate
> 7 critic
> 8 controversial /ˌkɒn.trəˈvɜː.ʃəl/

Optional activity

To help learners remember which words are spelled with p and b, display the following words from the text: *homeopathy, therapy, placebo, patient, practitioner, proponent, supporter, proof, belief, spend, company, popular, benefit.* Alternatively, you could say the words and learners find them in the text. Learners look at the words and count how many examples of *p* (14) there are in the words and how many examples of *b* (3). Remove the displayed words and ask learners to close their books. Show them the following gapped words and ask them to complete them adding *p* or *b*:

homeo_athy   thera_y   _lace_o   _atient   _ractitioner

_ro_onent   _roof   _elief   com_any   _o_ular   _enefit

Say the words or give clues to the meanings, if necessary.

Alternatively, you could ask learners to learn the words and do this at the beginning of the next lesson. Learners read the text to check their answers.

WHILE READING

READING FOR DETAIL

4 👤 Focus learners on the statements and remind them of the difference between *false* and *does not say* (See Unit 1 notes, page 14). Check that learners understand that *currently* means *now*. Learners complete the exercise. They compare answers, saying what is wrong with the false statements. Check answers with the class.

> ### Answers
>
> 1 F (Most health systems use conventional medicine.) 2 T 3 T 4 T 5 DNS 6 F (It was founded in 1948.) 7 DNS 8 T

IDENTIFYING OPINIONS

5 👤👥 Remind learners that Abigail Hayes is a Professional homeopath and Piers Wehner is a NHS General Practitioner. Focus learners on the first statement. Ask which of the writers is most likely to believe that a patient should have gone to see a doctor earlier. Show learners that they should put a tick in the *Piers Wehner* column. Check learners understand *side effects* (an unpleasant effect of a drug that happens in addition to the main, positive effect), *clinical trials* (scientific tests to discover if a medical treatment is effective) and *healing powers* (the ability to make an illness better). Learners continue working alone. They compare with a partner. Check answers with the class.

> ### Answers
>
> 1 Piers Wehner 2 Abigail Hayes 3 Piers Wehner
> 4 Abigail Hayes 5 Abigail Hayes 6 Abigail Hayes
> 7 Piers Wehner 8 Piers Wehner

READING BETWEEN THE LINES

6 👥 Learners discuss possible reasons for the statements from the text with a partner. They will need to use their own ideas and knowledge to do this. They compare answers with another pair. Check answers with the class.

> ### Possible answers
>
> 1 Conventional medicine is very expensive because it needs a great deal of testing and the pharmaceutical companies want to make a large profit. Surgery is also expensive as it is very complex.
> 2 There is no evidence that homeopathy works. Money is needed for other types of treatment.
> 3 There is a great deal of evidence to show that if people believe they are being cured, they get better. This is called *the placebo effect*. People are less stressed if they believe that they are well.
> 4 People may be less worried if they have shared their medical problems and know that somebody is looking after them. They may also be more motivated to look after themselves.
> 5 Clinical trials are expensive and homeopaths may not have the money or resources to test their medicines.

6 Conventional medicine is based on science. Doctors also have to prove that they are not wasting money when using homeopathy.

DISCUSSION

Learners discuss the questions in pairs or small groups. Give them a few minutes to think about their opinions and any language they may need to express them before they start speaking. Monitor to help with vocabulary and to encourage participation. Check a few answers with the class. Encourage learners to respond to each other's ideas.

Answers will vary.

READING 2

PREPARING TO READ

UNDERSTANDING KEY VOCABULARY

1 Learners complete the sentences with words from the box, using dictionaries if necessary. Learners compare with a partner. Check answers with the class.

Answers

1 burden 2 treatment 3 regardless 4 safety net
5 consultation 6 deducted 7 labour costs 8 premium

2 Learners discuss the questions. Tell them that this is a chance to discuss their own opinions. They will probably be expected to do this at an English-speaking university. Monitor to help with vocabulary and to encourage participation. Check a few answers with the class.

3 Learners read the questions and then the text to answer them. They compare answers with a partner. Check some answers with the class. Answers will depend on the country or countries that learners come from and their opinions in the last exercise. If all your learners are the same nationality, it will be useful to know something about that country's healthcare system.

WHILE READING

READING FOR DETAIL

4 Learners read the descriptions of the five healthcare systems and match them to the three types of system mentioned in the text: free, private or mixed. Learners compare with a partner. Check answers with the class.

Answers

1 free 2 private 3 free 4 private 5 mixed

SCANNING TO FIND KEY WORDS

5 Learners scan through the text highlighting appropriate words. They write them in the table. Learners compare answers. Check answers with the class. Learners record useful synonyms if appropriate.

Answers

synonyms of *people*	*residents, citizens, workers, patients, individuals*
synonyms of *money*	*taxes, income, contribution, costs, funding, salaries, profit*
related to *health*	*healthcare, consultations, medicines, hospitals, medical services, health insurance, medical costs, preventative medicine, infectious diseases*

READING BETWEEN THE LINES

6 Learners decide which statements are true. They compare answers, justifying their choices. Check answers with the class.

Answers

1 b The writer presents a balanced view of the different systems in the text, giving the advantages and disadvantages of all three.
2 a The essay provides a brief outline of the systems, and does not give detail about different countries or exactly what healthcare is covered.

DISCUSSION

7 Learners discuss the questions in pairs or small groups. Give them a few minutes to think about their opinions and any language

they may need to express them before they start speaking. Monitor to help with vocabulary and to encourage participation. Check a few answers with the class. Encourage learners to respond to each other's ideas.

Answers will vary.

LANGUAGE DEVELOPMENT

MEDICAL VOCABULARY

1 Learners match the words and collocations with the definitions, using dictionaries if necessary. Learners compare answers. Check answers with the class. Model and drill as necessary. Learners record useful words.

Answers
1 d 2 f 3 a 4 c 5 b 6 e 7 g

2 Learners read the sentences and complete them with the words from Exercise 1. Remind them that they may have to change the form of a word to make the sentence grammatically correct. Learners compare with a partner. Check answers with the class.

Answers
1 disease epidemic 2 underfunding 3 Drug dependency 4 sedentary lifestyle 5 preventable illness 6 patents 7 cosmetic surgery

ACADEMIC VOCABULARY

3 Draw learners' attention to the fact that the words in this exercise will be useful for a range of subjects, not just those related to health. Point out that the meaning of the adjective and the related noun are given. First they try writing the adjectives without a dictionary and then refer to one to check their answers. Learners compare answers. Check answers with the class.

Answers
1 adverse 2 professional 3 illegal 4 physical 5 complex 6 adequate 7 conventional 8 precise 9 medical

Optional activity

Ask learners what words 2, 3, 4, 7 and 9 have in common. They all end in the sound /l/ and all end in the letters -al. Point out that academic adjectives that end with this sound usually end with the letters -al. Ask learners to think of more or look through a text related to their field of study and find more -al words. Learners record them.

4 Learners work alone to complete the sentences by choosing one of the academic adjectives given from the two options. Learners compare answers. Check answers with the class. Learners record useful words.

Answers
1 illegal 2 professional 3 adequate 4 conventional 5 complex 6 physical 7 adverse 8 medical 9 precise

CRITICAL THINKING

Give learners a minute to read the Writing task they will do at the end of the unit (an essay, 'Avoiding preventative illness is the responsibility of individuals and their families, not governments.' Do you agree?) and keep it in mind as they do the next exercises.

EVALUATE

1 Learners work in small groups. They look at the list of actions that people can take to avoid getting ill and discuss which are the most useful. They try to agree on five.

2 In the same groups, learners answer the two questions about the five actions they chose.

Check a few answers with the class. Encourage learners to note down each other's ideas that they may want to use in their own essays.

UNDERSTAND

3 Learners read each statement and decide which ones suggest that the speaker is in favour of the individual taking responsibility for preventative healthcare and which ones are against it.

Do the first one or two statements together with the class. Then learners continue the exercise alone. Learners compare answers. Check answers with the class.

WRITING

GRAMMAR FOR WRITING

Optional lead-in

Focus learners on the first two paragraphs of Reading 2 on page 58. They highlight all the articles (definite and indefinite) that they can find (6 x *the*, 4 x *a* and 1 x *an*). Elicit some reasons for using definite and indefinite articles. Alternatively use a short text related to learners' academic subject(s) to do this.

ARTICLES

1 👤👥 Read out or paraphrase the information in the box. For each statement learners try to think of an example in English and decide whether the usage is the same in their language (if their language has articles).

Learners match the rules with the sentences. They compare with a partner. Check answers with the class.

Answers

1 f 2 d 3 h 4 b 5 g 6 c 7 e and a.

2 👤👥 Learners complete the sentences, referring back to the statements about article usage. They compare with a partner. Check answers with the class.

Answers

(Letters show which article usage statement applies.)
1 When travelling, it's usually easier to carry – (g) pills than *a* (e) bottle of medicine.
2 (f) Alternative medicine is popular in – (h) China.
3 *The* (c) first time I was in hospital was in 2010.
4 *The* (d) best facility in my city is *the* (b) Royal Hospital.
5 However, – (f) further research into *the* (a) specific area may be necessary.
6 It can be argued that – (f) homeopathy does no harm as *an* (e) additional service.
7 (f) Cost-effectiveness is *an* (e) important issue in healthcare.
8 (f) Homeopathy is *an* (e) ancient system of – (f) medicine.

LANGUAGE OF CONCESSION

3 👤👥 Remind learners that in Reading 2 the author had a strong opinion on the topic but also mentioned arguments that opposed their overall view. Ask why the author did this (It is important to acknowledge opposing views so that you can say why you disagree with them, which makes your own arguments stronger). Learners read the first paragraph of the box. Point out the following, if necessary:

- *However* is more formal than *but* and usually comes at the beginning of a sentence, followed by a comma.
- The difference between *nevertheless* and *however* is subtle. Both show some kind of contrast or concession. *Nevertheless* is used when the statement following it has a direct correlation with the statement before it. For example, *people still use it* refers to the fact that *Homeopathy seems to be ineffective*. If the second statement was, for example, *massage is more effective*, we would link the statements with *however*, because it is about a different subject.
- *Even though* is similar to *although* but suggests a greater element of surprise.
- *Despite* and *in spite of* have the same meaning and are both followed by nouns, pronouns or noun phrases. If the writer wants to follow either of these with a clause, *the fact that* needs to be used before the clause.
- Clauses of concession beginning with *nevertheless* or *however* need to come after the main clause. Clauses of concession with other linkers can come first or second. The final sentence could also be written as *People still use homeopathy, even though it seems to be ineffective*.

Learners rewrite the sentences using the prompts. Do a sentence together with the class as an example. Weaker learners could discuss these together but write them individually. Monitor closely to help with language and content. Learners compare with a partner. Check answers with the class. Although there are different possible answers, ensure that the end of the sentence has an appropriate concession.

1 Conventional medicine is effective even though it may have unpleasant side effects.

2 Many people argue that homeopathy should be part of the health service. However, critics argue that it denies other people proven treatments.

3 Homeopathy is a popular choice for many in spite of the fact that there is no scientific evidence that it works.

4 Ayurveda is still commonly practised in the twenty-first century, despite the fact that it is 3,500 years old.

5 The British Medical Association is opposed to the state funding of homeopathy but the Government is still considering funding it.

6 Many people think homeopathy does not work. Nevertheless, people should have the right to access it if they believe it works.

ACADEMIC WRITING SKILLS

WRITING AN INTRODUCTION TO AN ESSAY (2)

1 👤👥 Go through the information in the box with the class. Point out that an introduction does not need to include all of the features mentioned. Learners read the introduction and identify which of the features in the box are used. Learners compare with a partner. Check answers with the class.

Answers
1 a 2 c 3 b

2 👤👥 Focus learners on the essay title. Check they understand the title fully by asking the following questions:

- Do you write about ways to cure these diseases? (No, about avoiding them.)
- Do you write about health generally? (No, just preventable illnesses.)
- Do you write about your own government? (You can mention it if you wish, but the question is about governments in general.)
- Do you need to write an equally balanced argument in favour of either individuals or governments taking responsibility for preventable illnesses? (No, you can take one side, but you should also mention some arguments for the opposing view.)
- Where will you find background information on the topic? (In this unit, especially in the Critical thinking section. You should also use your own opinions.)

Learners plan out the introduction to their essay by writing one sentence in each section of the table. Remind them that when defining the topic they should not repeat the question; they need to paraphrase it. Learners compare their sentences and help each other to improve them. Remind them that when they write the whole essay, they will need to link these to make the paragraph more fluent.

WRITING TASK

WRITING A FIRST DRAFT

1 👤 Focus learners on the writing task. Check they understand the title fully. Learners make notes using the plan provided. They do not write full sentences here, only notes of the information and ideas they wish to include. For the introduction they can use the sentences from the Academic Writing Skills section, but may not wish to use all of them. In the conclusion they need to say whether they believe governments or individuals should take the responsibility for avoiding preventable illnesses. If they believe the responsibility should be shared they should say how. Give learners the opportunity to ask you questions about vocabulary or use dictionaries. Tell them they will not be allowed to use a dictionary while they are writing.

2 👤 Learners write the first draft of their essay following their plans. Allow about 40 minutes for this. They should write at least 250 words and highlight any language (including spelling) of which they are unsure. Give them a warning five minutes before the end of the set time.

EDIT

3 👤 To encourage learners to take responsibility for their own learning, tell them to check their writing using the task checklist. Stress that this is a very important part of the writing process as it helps learners to learn from their mistakes. Encourage them to look back over their plan and at the unit.

4 👤 Learners make any necessary changes to their essay.

5 👤 Learners check their written language using the language checklist. They can also check any spelling that they were unsure of by looking back over the unit, using a dictionary,

or by asking other learners or you. In addition, remind them to check carefully for any errors that they often make in their writing (e.g. particular spellings, subject-verb agreements, omitting verbs, etc.)

6 👤👥 Learners make any other changes and write up their final drafts. If comfortable doing so, they can read each other's writing and suggest improvements before handing the essays in to you for marking.

OBJECTIVES REVIEW

See Introduction, page 9 for ideas about using the Objectives review with your learners.

WORDLIST

See Introduction, page 9 for ideas about how to make the most of the Wordlist with your learners.

REVIEW TEST

See page 101 for the photocopiable Review test for this unit and page 92 for ideas about when and how to administer the Review test.

MODEL ANSWER

See page 127 for the photocopiable Model answer.

RESEARCH PROJECT

Create a website describing how medicine has changed over time.

Explain to the class that they are going to research how medicine has changed over time which could include nutrition, surgery, the diagnosis and treatment of diseases, preventive medicine, or another field of the learners' choice.

Learners should be encouraged to find out about traditional remedies as well as modern medicine. They could find science journals and websites for information or interview elderly family members. Alternatively they could make videos and pictures and recordings to populate their website.

4 RISK

Learning objectives

Focus learners on the Learning objectives box and tell them that this is what they will be working on in this unit. Later they will write an essay: *'If children are never exposed to risk they will never be able to cope with risk. Give reasons for and against this statement and give your opinion.'* Show learners this essay title on page 83 but reassure them that all the work in this unit will help them to write it. At the end of the unit they will be able to assess how well they can manage the skills in the Learning objectives box.

UNLOCK YOUR KNOWLEDGE

Lead-in

Ask learners to write the word *risk* vertically on a piece of paper. Elicit a word beginning with *r* that they think could be risky, e.g. *rollerblading*. Ask why they chose this word. In pairs they then continue and write one word for each of the other letters (*i, s* and *k*). They must be able to justify why their choices could be risky. The first pair to finish tell the others their words and justify them. They are the winners if the majority of the others agree with their justifications. Otherwise the next pair give their answers. Some suggestions are: *i: Internet, insect bites, s: smoking, sunburn, k: kidnapping, knives.*

1 Focus learners on the list of activities. Check they understand the difference between *doing housework* (cleaning the house, etc) and *doing homework* (studying at home). In pairs they discuss if the activities are low risk, high risk or extremely high risk. Learners compare answers with another pair. Check with the class – there are no right or wrong answers.

2 In groups, learners discuss what could be done to make each activity safer. For example, if you go rock climbing you should have all the correct equipment, go with an experienced rock climber, practise on a climbing wall first, etc. If you want to make the activity shorter, ask learners to choose five of the activities to discuss. Monitor to help with language and encourage participation. Check some ideas with the class.

3 Learners discuss the questions in pairs or small groups. Monitor to help with language and encourage participation. Invite learners to share some ideas with the class.

Optional activity

Learners highlight all the words in the list of activities in Ex 1 that end with *-ing* and write the base form (infinitive) of each verb. They tick the base forms that have *-ing* added to the whole word, e.g. *climb* and compare the ones they have ticked with the others. Ask if they can see any patterns in the words (those verbs ending in *e*, such as *ride*, drop the *e* before adding *-ing*). Elicit or remind learners that one-syllable words ending *cvc* (consonant vowel consonant) and words of more than one syllable in which the final *cvc* is stressed double the final consonant before adding *-ing*. In American English the *-ing* form *traveling* is spelled with one *l*, but in British English words ending in *l* are usually doubled, e.g. *cancelling, labelling, signalling*. Give learners two or three minutes to scan through this unit to find some other words ending with *-ing*. Ask them to identify which pattern they follow.

WATCH AND LISTEN

Video script

ROLLER COASTERS

Narrator: Why do we find it fun to scare ourselves on rollercoasters? All over the world people love rollercoasters. The twists, turns, ups and downs at speed are all disorientating and at times uncomfortable. Yet when we get off the ride we feel great and cannot wait to get on again.

Throughout history human beings have often found themselves at risk being hunted by wild animals such as wolves, victims of natural disasters or subjected to harsh weather.

In extreme circumstances with stress, fear or pain, the body produces natural chemicals. The hormone adrenalin helps the body perform better meaning people are more alert and able to run faster or are stronger. Additionally the body's natural painkillers, endorphins are produced. These not only help the body withstand pain and discomfort, but also make people feel good.

Rollercoasters trick the body into feeling fear, and so into producing endorphins. This enables people to experience exhilaration without putting themselves in serious danger. There are strict controls on the design and forces which can be used on rollercoasters during the planning stage and meticulous safety checks and inspections are carried out daily once the ride is built. In the modern world we have developed ways to experience danger and push our bodies to the limits to generate the feeling of exhilaration.

This might be cave diving at a depth of 400 feet, sledging in the snow, driving fast cars, running with bulls, or aerobatics in small planes.

Rollercoasters, however, are perhaps the most accessible form of thrills. The advantage of rollercoasters is that they change the way the body feels with rapid results and they offer thrills without risk.

PREPARING TO WATCH

USING YOUR KNOWLEDGE TO PREDICT CONTENT

1 👥 Focus learners on the pictures and the questions. Learners discuss the questions in pairs. Check a few answers with the class – there are no right or wrong answers.

UNDERSTANDING KEY VOCABULARY

2 👤👥 Learners read the sentences and decide if each adjective is positive or negative, using the context of the sentences to help them. Learners compare answers. Check answers with the class. The prefixes *dis-* and *un-* may hint at negative meanings. Model and drill the pronunciation of exhilarating and disorientating.

> **Answers**
>
> Positive adjectives: exhilarating, thrilling
> Negative adjectives: disorientating, harsh, uncontrolled

3 👤👥 Learners match the adjectives to the definitions. There are two answers for the first definition. They compare answers in pairs. Check answers with the class.

> **Answers**
>
> 1 exhilarating, thrilling 2 harsh 3 disorientating
> 4 uncontrolled

WHILE WATCHING

UNDERSTANDING MAIN IDEAS

4 ▶️👤 Tell learners they are going to watch a video about why people take risks. Learners watch and compare the information in the video to their answers to the two questions in Exercise 1. Learners compare answers. Check a few answers with the class. Focus learners on the pictures and elicit or give the activities shown (cave diving, rollercoaster, driving fast cars, running with bulls, plane acrobatics). Ask which one of the activities in the pictures above the video mainly focused on (rollercoasters, although all were mentioned).

UNDERSTANDING DETAIL

5 👥 👥👥 Focus learners on the beginnings of the sentences. In pairs they spend a few minutes trying to complete them according to the information in the video. Learners compare answers with another pair. Tell them that they will watch the video again soon to check their answers.

6 👤👥👥 Learners look at the diagram. Help them to understand it by asking these questions:

- What does the diagram show? (The physical and chemical effects on the body in extreme circumstances.)
- On the second level of the diagram, why are there two pieces of information? (Because there are two possible effects.)
- Which word from the box completes number 1 on the diagram? (adrenalin)

  Learners complete the diagram using the words in the box. They compare answers in pairs. Again tell them that they will watch the video to check them. Model and drill the word *alert* [/əˈlɜːt/]. Play the video again. While they are watching tell learners they should just listen, as if they are busy writing one answer they may not hear the next piece of information they need. Stop the video sometimes if you like to let them write, but do not continue until everyone is watching.

RESPONDING TO THE VIDEO CONTENT

7 ▶️👥👥 Learners watch the video again to check their answers to Exercises 5 and 6. Check answers as a group after watching.

Suggested answers Exercise 5

1 ...they're disorientating and uncomfortable.
2 ... wild animals, natural disasters, and harsh weather.
3 ... they have daily safety inspections.
4 ... cave diving, sledging, driving fast cars, running with bulls, aerobatics.
5 ... they are exciting without being dangerous.

Answers Exercise 6

1 adrenalin 2 alert 3 faster 4 stronger 5 withstand pain 6 feel good

8 👥👥 Learners discuss the questions in groups. Give them a few minutes to think about their opinions and language they may need to express them before they start speaking. Monitor to help with vocabulary and to encourage participation.

DISCUSSION

9 👥 👥👥 Learners discuss the questions in pairs or small groups. Give them a few minutes to think about their opinions and language they may need to express them before they start speaking. Monitor to help with vocabulary and to encourage participation. Check a few answers with the class. Encourage learners to respond to each other's ideas.

Answers will vary.

READING 1

PREPARING TO READ

UNDERSTANDING KEY VOCABULARY

1 👤👥 Learners match the words and phrases to the definitions, using dictionaries if necessary. Alternatively, they could try the reading the quiz in Exercise 3 first and then do this exercise, so they can guess the answers from context. Learners compare answers. Check answers with the class.

Answers
1 f 2 a 3 c 4 g 5 b 6 d 7 e

PREVIEWING THE TOPIC

2 👥 Paraphrase or ask learners to read the information in the box. Point out that the reading in this section is not as academic as some of the other texts but is a way of getting learners to explore their own ideas on the topic that they will be writing about later. Learners discuss the questions with a partner. Before they do this ask if they can guess the meaning of averse /əˈvɜːs/ from the sentence (a strong dislike or opposition to something). Ask the learners for some of their ideas but do not give any answers at this stage.

WHILE READING

3 👤 Focus learners on the quiz and point out that their answers should not be taken too seriously. They read the quiz and mark their responses to the questions. Encourage them to guess unknown vocabulary rather than use dictionaries at this stage.

READING FOR MAIN IDEAS

4 👥 Learners compare and discuss their answers. They also say what they think the difference is between a, b and c answers. What do they think their answers suggest about their attitude to risk? Remind them that this quiz is just for fun.

5 👤👥 Learners read the explanations of the answers and complete them with the letters a, b or c based on the discussion they had in Exercise 3. They compare answers. Check answers with the class. At this stage you could also check and discuss learners' answers to Exercise 2.

Answers
1 b 2 c 3 a

READING FOR DETAIL

6 👤 Learners match the phrases with the a, b and c answers in the quiz. Go through the first example, eliciting why this is the correct answer. With a weaker group, do a few more examples. Allow use of a dictionary if necessary. Learners compare with a partner. Check answers with the class.

Answers
1 2 a 2 4 a 3 3 c 4 1 c 5 6 b 6 5 a 7 7 a

Optional activity

If you focused on the spelling of words with -ing at the beginning of the unit, learners could find more -ing words here and in the quiz and account for their spellings.

READING BETWEEN THE LINES

7 ⚎ Learners discuss the questions, referring back to the text if necessary. Point out that they should use their own ideas and knowledge here. They compare answers with another pair. Check answers with the class. Remember there are no right or wrong answers.

> ### Possible answers
>
> 1 It could be dangerous if you get very excited and you have heart problems.
> 2 You have more control over how the money is used and you help your family.
> 3 You might be late for something important one day.
> 4 Sailing around the world is very expensive, time consuming and risky.
> 5 It takes too long and you read a lot of unnecessary information.
> 6 You could get some strange food which you might not like.
> 7 The job is usually easy and risk-free, but check-in clerks probably get discounted air travel.

DISCUSSION

8 ⚎⚎ Learners discuss the questions in pairs or small groups. Monitor to help with vocabulary and to encourage participation. Check a few answers with the class. Encourage learners to respond to each other's ideas.

> Answers will vary.

READING 2

PREPARING TO READ

USING YOUR KNOWLEDGE TO PREDICT CONTENT

1 ⚎ Learners discuss the questions. If they are from the same country, it may be more interesting for them to talk about other countries they know. As they may then be able to make comparisons with their own country. If you have a multi-national class, try to pair learners from different countries. Check a few answers with the class.

> Answers will vary.

UNDERSTANDING KEY VOCABULARY

2 ⚎⚎ Learners complete the definitions with the words in the box, using dictionaries if necessary. Learners compare with a partner. Check answers with the class.

> ### Answers
>
> 1 compulsory 2 infringe 3 Prudence 4 Legislation 5 prohibiting 6 responsibility 7 Regulations

3 ⚎⚎ Learners discuss the issues, saying whether they think governments should control these. They should be prepared to justify their opinions and give examples. Monitor to help with vocabulary and to encourage participation. Check a few answers with the class, asking for justifications.

WHILE READING

READING FOR MAIN IDEAS

4 ⚎⚎ Tell learners that they are going to read an essay about the question they have just been discussing. Allow them a few minutes to read the essay and find out which of the issues they discussed in Exercise 3 are mentioned. Discourage dictionary use at this stage. Warn learners that the issues may be paraphrased. Learners compare with a partner. Check answers with the class.

> ### Answers
>
> Issues mentioned: 2, 4, 5, 8, 9

SCANNING TO FIND INFORMATION

5 ⚎ Learners scan the text to find the words given, then look for a synonym for each word in the text. Do the first one together as an example (countries is in Line 1. Nations in Line 6 is a synonym). Tell learners there may be more than one possible synonym for each word in the text. Learners compare with a partner. Check answers with the class.

> ### Answers
>
> 1 countries; nations 2 injury; harm 3 people; citizens; the population; the public; society 4 financial; economic 5 regulations; legislation 6 liable; responsible

READING BETWEEN THE LINES

MAKING INFERENCES FROM THE TEXT

6 Learners discuss the questions, referring back to the text and using their own knowledge. Check answers with the class.

Possible answers

1 They may not be so careful about protecting their workers' safety.
2 Paying fines for riding a motorbike without a helmet.
3 Restrictions on workers' hours and duties, need for safety equipment, etc.
4 Probably not. The writer says 'a country with tight controls provides a pleasant and safe environment'.

DISCUSSION

7 Learners discuss the questions in pairs or small groups. Give them a few minutes to think about their opinions and any language they may need to express them before they start speaking. Monitor to help with vocabulary and to encourage participation. Check a few answers with the class. Encourage learners to respond to each other's ideas.

Answers will vary.

⊙ LANGUAGE DEVELOPMENT

LANGUAGE OF FREEDOM

1 Ensure learners understand the difference between *promote freedom* (encourage it) and *restrict freedom* (not completely allow it). Point out that the words in the box are all verbs, although some of them (*ban, limit, permit, grant*) are also nouns. Learners put the words they already know into the appropriate column of the table, then use a dictionary to check the others if necessary. Learners compare answers. Check answers with the class. Learners record useful words.

Answers

Promoting freedom: allow; legalize; permit; authorize; grant
Restricting freedom: ban; limit; restrict; criminalize; curb

2 Learners decide which of the three given words (*a, b* or *c*) complete the sentences. They compare with a partner. Check answers with the class.

Answers

1 b *ban* (you usually *grant the right* to do something, *restrict* means a partial limit and so cannot be used with *completely*)
2 a *authorize* (*criminalize* and *legalize* refer to a general activity, not a specific project)
3 b *criminalize* (*criminalize* means to make something illegal)
4 a *limit* (*ban* would be complete, *limit* is partial; we follow *legalize* with a noun, not *on*)
5 a *grant* (*grant the right to* do something)

ACADEMIC NOUNS

3 Paraphrase or ask learners to read the information in the box. Some learners try to avoid using long words as they find them more difficult to spell, but reassure them that academic words are usually spelled more regularly than some shorter, more common ones. They can also relate the spelling to similar words and learn some common word endings like *-tion* and *-sion*. The ending *-tion* is much more common; *-sion* is usually used to turn a verb ending in *s* or *d* into a noun: *conclude → conclusion, revise → revision* etc. Learners replace the nouns in bold with the words in the box. Model and drill the word *chaos* /ˈkeɪ.ɒ/. Learners compare answers. Check answers with the class. Learners record useful words.

Answers

1 reduction 2 legislation 3 prevention 4 dissatisfaction 5 regulation(s) 6 confusion 7 objection

CRITICAL THINKING

Give learners a minute to read the Writing task they will do at the end of the unit (a for and against essay, *If children are never exposed to risk, they will never be able to cope with risk. Discuss the arguments for and against this statement and give your opinion.*) and keep it in mind as they do the next exercises.

EVALUATE

1 👤👥 Focus learners on the list of risks. Check meaning of *get-rich-quick schemes* (opportunities to make a great deal of money very quickly, which are very often illegal or fraudulent), and *risk assessment* (the process of finding out how much risk is involved in a particular situation). Learners categorize the list of risks into personal, professional and financial. Some may fall into more than one category. Learners compare with a partner. Check answers with the class.

> **Answers**
>
> 1 financial 2 professional /personal 3 personal/professional 4 financial 5 personal/professional/financial 6 professional 7 professional 8 financial 9 financial/personal 10 personal/professional 11 financial 12 personal

APPLY

2 👤👥 Although the activities in Exercise 2 involve risks, they may also offer rewards. Learners match the rewards in the list to the risks above. Check understanding of *maximizing profit* (earning as much money as possible). Learners compare with a partner. Check answers with the class.

> **Answers**
>
> 1 a 2 d 3 g 4 j 5 k 6 l 7 c 8 i 9 f 10 e 11 h 12 b

3 👥 Learners now use their own ideas to discuss reasons for not taking the risks in Exercise 2. To save time, you could ask learners to only choose six that they want to discuss or you could set a time limit. Monitor to help with language and encourage participation. Learners share their ideas. Encourage them to react to each other's opinions and note down interesting ones as these may be useful when writing their essays.

> **Possible answers**
>
> 1 You could lose all your money.
> 2 You could be injured.
> 3 You could break something or make it incorrectly.
> 4 You might have to pay a large fine from the tax office.
> 5 You might get arrested and go to prison.
> 6 Somebody might get injured.
> 7 You might get disciplined or even fired.
> 8 You could find yourself with no money for necessities.

> 9 You might not be able to replace valuable items if your house was burgled.
> 10 You could be delayed if you miss a train or plane.
> 11 You might not have the money to pay for the things you bought on credit at a later date.
> 12 You could get seriously injured in a car accident.

> **Optional activity**
>
> Learners think about three or four risks related to their own field of study. In pairs, they discuss one reward and one danger for each of these. Encourage learners to share their ideas with the class.

WRITING

GRAMMAR FOR WRITING

CAUSE AND EFFECT

1 👤👥 Check learners understand the difference between cause and effect. Put something (unbreakable) on the table and push it off so it falls on the floor. Elicit the cause and effect in this situation. Paraphrase or ask learners to read the information in the box. Focus learners on the first sentence in Exercise 1 and ask them how to complete it using one of the verb phrases from the box. Learners complete the other two sentences. There is more than one possible answer in each case. Learners compare with a partner. Check answers with the class.

> **Possible answers**
>
> 1 Taking fewer risks leads to smaller rewards.
> 2 Managing risk carefully means everybody stays safer.
> 3 Excessive risk-taking may result in chaos.

2 👤👥 Learners complete the sentences using their own ideas about results. They compare with a partner. Check answers with the class.

> **Possible answers**
>
> 1 Some people avoid paying tax to save money. Consequently, the government has less money to spend on essential services.
> 2 Many groups have criticized banks' excessive risk taking. As a result of this, some financial institutions have adopted less risky strategies.
> 3 It is very difficult to predict how long the bus will take to get to the station. Because of this, it is advisable to allow plenty of time for the journey.

CONDITIONAL LANGUAGE

3 👤👥 Ask learners a question such as *Should employees be fired for turning up late for work?* Try to elicit conditions in their answers, e.g. *They should only be fired if they are usually late.* Paraphrase or ask learners to read the information in the box. Learners complete each sentence using one of the linkers from the box and their own ending. Encourage them to use all of the linkers if possible. Stronger learners could rewrite some of the sentences, putting the linkers first. Learners compare with a partner. Check answers with the class. Accept all reasonable ideas but make sure learners use the linkers correctly, following them with a complete conditional clause.

> ### Possible answers
>
> 1 Individuals should be allowed to do whatever they like as long as they do not harm anybody.
> 2 Risk is acceptable in the workplace provided that suitable precautions have been taken.
> 3 Potential problems connected to risk-taking can be minimized provided that a proper risk assessment is done before any activity.
> 4 Financial investments do not need to be risky provided that good advice is sought first.

ACADEMIC WRITING SKILLS

TOPIC SENTENCES IN BODY PARAGRAPHS

1 👤👥 Paraphrase or ask learners to read the information in the box. Learners then choose the correct words to complete the sentences. They compare with a partner. Check answers with the class.

> ### Answers
>
> 1 main idea
> 2 general (It gives an overview of what is in that paragraph and is usually followed by more specific examples or details.)
> 3 no (Generally a topic sentence does not give any examples to back up a point.)

2 👥 Remembering the advice given in Exercise 1, learners decide which is the best option in each pair of topic sentences, *a* or *b*. Do the first one together as an example. Learners compare with a partner. Check answers with the class.

> ### Answers
>
> 1 a This sentence is more general and tells us what the paragraph is going to be about. Sentence b is too specific.
> 2 a Sentence b is too short and does not tell us what the paragraph is about.
> 3 b Sentence a gives a very specific example which is not suitable for a topic sentence.
> 4 a Sentence b does not give the main theme of the paragraph.

WRITING TASK

WRITING A FIRST DRAFT

1 👤 Focus learners on the writing task. Check they understand the title fully by asking the following questions:

- Does the statement (the first part of the essay title) encourage or discourage exposing children to some risk? (It encourages it.)
- Can you write about adults in the essay? (Only in terms of children when they grow up.)
- Do you need to use an equal balance of advantages and disadvantages in the essay? (Yes, in the body of the essay you should address both sides equally.)
- In which part of the essay will you give your own opinion? (In the conclusion.)
- Where will you find background information, appropriate language and some opinions? (In this unit, and use your own opinions.)

2 👤 Learners now make notes on the supporting evidence for their essay. They do not have to write full sentences here, but they should consider any language that they think they will need. Give learners the opportunity to ask you questions about vocabulary or use dictionaries. Tell them they will not be allowed to use dictionaries while they are writing.

Give learners some time to look back over the unit to identify three arguments for and three arguments against the statement. They could do this in pairs. If they are struggling you could ask some of the following questions:

- Is it possible to protect children from all risks?
- Do you need to take risks in order to learn?
- Whose role is it to protect children?
- To what extent can children assess risks for themselves?
- Do children usually like to experiment and take risks?

- What are the short-term and long-term risks of playing computer games, going to the beach, playing football, travelling in a car, playing on an adventure playground?
- How can the risks in the last question be reduced?

3 ⌂ Learners write one sentence giving their overall opinion which will be the topic sentence for their conclusion. Remind them to use conditional language if appropriate. Then they make notes of some supporting evidence for this opinion.

4 ⌂ Learners write the first draft of their essay following their plans. Allow about 40 minutes for this. They should write at least 250 words and highlight any language (including spelling) of which they are unsure. Give them a warning five minutes before the end of the set time.

EDIT

5 ⌂ To encourage learners to take responsibility for their own learning, tell them to check their writing using the task checklist. Stress that this is a very important part of the writing process as it helps learners to learn from their mistakes. Encourage them to look back over their plan and at the unit.

6 ⌂ Learners make any necessary changes to their essay.

7 ⌂ Learners check their written language now using the checklist. They can also check any spelling that they were unsure of by looking back over the unit, using a dictionary, or by asking other learners or you. In addition, remind them to check carefully for any errors that they often make in their writing (e.g. particular spellings, subject-verb agreements, omitting verbs, etc.)

8 ⌂⌂⌂ Learners make any other changes and write up their final drafts. If comfortable doing so, they can read each other's writing and suggest improvements before handing the essays in to you for marking.

OBJECTIVES REVIEW

See Introduction, page 9 for ideas about using the Objectives review with your learners.

WORDLIST

See Introduction, page 9 for ideas about how to make the most of the Wordlist with your learners.

REVIEW TEST

See page 95 for the photocopiable Review test for this unit and page 92 for ideas about when and how to administer the Review test.

MODEL ANSWER

See page 128 for the photocopiable Model answer.

RESEARCH PROJECT

Evaluate the risk in different jobs and find out which one is the riskiest.

Divide the class into groups. Each group researches a different job, from the following: fisherman, sportsperson, police officer, scientist, driver, nurse, farmer and pilot.

Each group researches aspects of their given job like: how much people are paid, risks and benefits, typical duties of the job and qualifications and skills needed. Learners could contact someone who does their given job and interview them.

Each group presents the job they have researched and decide on which the riskiest one is and why.

5 MANUFACTURING

UNLOCK YOUR KNOWLEDGE

Lead-in

Tell learners that you are thinking of a product or raw material and they have to ask you *yes/no* questions to find out what it is. They can only ask 20 questions about each product. Elicit a few sample questions (e.g. *Is it produced in this country? Is it manufactured? Is it something we use every day? Can you eat it?*). Remind learners to listen carefully to each other's questions and answers so they do not waste questions by repeating them. If they ask questions to which you do not know the answers, tell them that you do not know but do not count that as one of the 20 questions. Start the game. Some example products you could use are: *rice, wool, steel, oil, leather, bread*. When they have guessed or reached 20 questions, continue the game if you wish by asking one learner to think of a product (or give them the name of one) and getting them to respond to other learners' questions.

1 Focus learners on the words in the box and ask when we use them (when describing a process, story, or something else where the order of events is important). Point out that *then*, *after that*, *next* and *later* can be used in any order. They are almost synonymous, but *later* suggests that some time has passed before this stage. The class works together to describe how to make a cup of coffee. Encourage use of the sequencing words. Learners do the rest of the exercise in pairs. Monitor and help with language where necessary. Check answers with the class.

Possible answers

2 First you need to walk to the end of the street and turn left. Then cross the road and walk to the bus stop. After that, you wait for a number 25 bus and when it comes, take it to the school. Finally, you need to get off the bus, cross the street and enter the school.

3 First you read the title and make sure you understand it. Next you decide what kind of essay it is. Then you make a plan. After that write some notes for each paragraph. Write your essay. Read and check it carefully before giving it to the teacher.

4 First you get a fish, cover it in flour or breadcrumbs, and then you fry it. After that you fry some chips. Finally, you boil some peas and then eat it all together.

5 First you need to find a suitable job on the Internet, in the newspaper or hear about it from somebody you know. Then you send in your application form and CV. Next, if you meet the criteria, you may be invited to an interview. Finally, if you are the best candidate, you will be offered the job.

2 Discuss the question with the class. If appropriate, ask learners when they would need to describe processes and sequences in their own field(s) of study.

Possible answers

Many different academic disciplines require you to be able to write in this kind of way, especially human and physical sciences, as the order in which things happen is important.

WATCH AND LISTEN

Video script

MAKING CHOCOLATE

Chocolate production begins with the harvesting of cocoa pods from trees. It is grown in rain forests in countries on the equator such as Ghana, Ivory Coast, Brazil and Indonesia. The pods contain beans which are fermented and dried in the sun for a week or more. At this stage the beans taste bitter and nothing like chocolate. Once dried, the beans are transported in large sacks and sold to chocolate producers all over the world.

In the chocolate factory, before production begins, a sample of beans is tested by splitting them so the inside is revealed. In a good bean, the insides are clearly separated. This shows that the fermentation has worked and has begun to remove the bean's natural bitterness. The beans are washed, then roasted. Roasting is the most important part of the process. It is critical that the beans are roasted at the correct temperature otherwise the taste is adversely affected.

As the beans are roasted, the amino acids and sugars found in the beans begin to react together to form the familiar chocolate flavour. The roasted beans are then shelled and the centre or 'nib' is what is left. The nibs need to go through a grinder to make them into a liquid. At this stage extra cocoa butter is added to help make the final chocolate texture as smooth as possible.

The next stage is when the chocolate liquid, milk and sugar, which are required to make chocolate, are mixed together. The resulting chocolate paste is then passed through rollers and turned into a powder. The chocolate powder is mixed with milk powder and heated. This is called conching and can last up to a week. The acidity helps turn the mixture into a liquid chocolate syrup. This is then tempered. Tempering is when the chocolate is heated, cooled and gradually heated again to a warm temperature. Tempering is the secret of quality chocolate. The change of temperature enables the fats to crystallize which results in large bars of chocolate. Industrial chocolate producers will then sell these slabs to chocolate specialists. The chocolate bars are melted again by tempering and then can be moulded to make individual chocolates. At this stage fillings can be added in between layers of chocolate. Finally, when the chocolates are finished they are left to set in trays ready to be packaged, sold and eaten.

PREPARING TO WATCH

USING YOUR KNOWLEDGE TO PREDICT CONTENT

1   Learners discuss the questions using their own knowledge. Check they understand the meaning of *artificial* (not natural). Check learners' ideas with the class, but do not give any answers yet.

UNDERSTANDING KEY VOCABULARY

2   Point out that the first column consists of verbs related to chocolate making. Learners match any verbs that they know or can guess first, then use a dictionary if necessary. Remind learners when using dictionaries that some of these words have several meanings and they will need to find the correct one (especially *mould*). Learners compare answers in pairs. Check answers with the class.

> **Answers**
> a 4 b 5 c 8 d 6 e 7 f 3 g 1 h 2

3   Learners discuss the most likely order of the verbs in the chocolate-making process by numbering them on a piece of paper or in their books.

4   Learners watch the video to check their predictions in Exercises 1 and 3. They compare answers in pairs. Check answers with the class.

> **Answers**
> 1 harvest 2 dry 3 roast 4 shell 5 grind 6 melt
> 7 mould 8 package

WHILE WATCHING

UNDERSTANDING DETAIL

5   Tell learners they are going to watch the video again. Ask them to look at the flow chart first and predict the answers (or try to remember them from the first viewing) in pairs. Learners watch the video to check their answers. They compare answers again. Check answers with the class.

> **Answers**
> 2 week 3 transported 4 roasted 5 shelled 6 butter
> 7 sugar 8 milk 9 heated 10 eaten

6   Learners match the stages and reasons. Check they understand *bitterness* by asking what can taste bitter (orange peel, some coffee) and checking they do not confuse it with *sour* tastes (like lemon and vinegar). Tell them that *tempering* is a process in chocolate making but they do not need to learn this word for general use. Learners compare answers in pairs. Check answers with the class.

> **Answers**
> 1 d 2 f 3 a 4 e 5 g 6 b 7 c

MAKING INFERENCES

7   Learners discuss the questions and choose the best answers. Point out that they need to use their own knowledge and logical thinking to answer these questions. Check answers with the class. Ask them to justify their answers, but point out that it does not matter if their answers are incorrect, as they are practising making inferences.

Answers

1 a 2 a 3 c

DISCUSSION

8 Learners discuss the questions in pairs or small groups. Give them a few minutes to think about their opinions and language they may need to express them before they start speaking. Monitor to help with vocabulary and to encourage participation. Check a few answers with the class. Encourage learners to respond to each other's ideas.

Answers will vary.

READING 1

PREPARING TO READ

Optional lead-in

Have a class discussion about silk to engage learners' interest and activate existing knowledge in the topic. Ask questions such as these:

- What adjectives do you think of when you think of silk?
- What are the special properties of silk?
- What kinds of things are made from silk nowadays? What about in the past?
- What do you know about the production of silk?
- What do you know about the history of silk?

ACTIVATING PRIOR KNOWLEDGE

1 Paraphrase or ask learners to read the information in the box. Learners then look at the table and complete the first two columns together. Listen to some answers from the class, asking learners to justify their ideas.

2 Learners read the text to check if their facts have been mentioned and write answers to their questions in the final column. They compare answers in pairs. Check answers with the class.

Answers will vary.

WHILE READING

3 Focus learners on the statements and remind them of the difference between *false* and *does not say*. Do one or two examples with the whole class, eliciting the reasons for the answers in the text. Learners complete the exercise. They compare answers, saying what is wrong with the false statements. Check answers with the class.

Answers

1 T 2 T 3 DNS 4 F (They can only eat mulberry leaves.) 5 DNS (People could be punished by death, but the text does not specify numbers.) 6 F (It is just as popular.) 7 DNS 8 T

4 Learners look at the multiple choice questions and try to answer them before consulting the text again. They compare answers in pairs. Check answers with the class.

Answers

1 d 2 a 3 d (The princess only took them to her own Asian province.) 4 c 5 d

READING BETWEEN THE LINES

INFERRING MEANING

5 In this activity learners need to think of reasons for information in the text. Do the first sentence together with the class. Learners could also discuss the questions first in groups. They write their answers either individually or in pairs. Learners compare answers in pairs, or in groups if they wrote the sentences in pairs. Check answers with the class.

Possible answers

1 *The writer says the history of silk has not been 'smooth' because...* the Chinese put people to death for passing on the means of making it.
2 *The Chinese were probably very protective of the silk manufacturing process because...*they wanted the rest of the world to trade with them and they would be able to set a high price for it.
3 *Although it was expensive, silk had probably 'become popular around the Mediterranean' because...*it was comfortable to wear in hot weather.
4 *Man-made fibres are cheaper and easier to manufacture because...*producers do not have to wait six weeks for silk worms to grow. It is a much less delicate manufacturing process.

DISCUSSION

6 👥 👥👥 Learners discuss the questions in pairs or small groups. Give them a few minutes to think about their opinions and language they may need to express them before they start speaking. Monitor to help with vocabulary and to encourage participation. Check a few answers with the class. Encourage learners to respond to each other's ideas.

> **Answers will vary.**

READING 2

PREPARING TO READ

USING YOUR KNOWLEDGE TO PREDICT CONTENT

> **Optional lead-in**
> Learners look around the room and name all the different items they can see that are made of paper.

1 👥 In pairs, learners brainstorm ideas about how paper is manufactured, its history and what it is used for. They write notes on the ideas map. They use dictionaries for any words or spellings they do not know. Check answers with the class, dealing with vocabulary and spelling issues. Avoid any detailed feedback on the manufacturing process, as this is the topic of the reading.

WHILE READING

READING FOR MAIN IDEAS

2 👤👥 The aim of this exercise is to help learners to see how much information they can find out from the first sentence of a paragraph. This can not only give them the main ideas of the whole text but also help them to find the most likely position for a specific piece of information. Make sure learners are aware of the difference between *raw materials* (materials in their natural state which have not yet been processed, such as wheat) and *products* (something made to be sold, such as bread). Learners read the four headings and the first sentence of each paragraph in order to match them, then write the sub-headings in the appropriate spaces in the text. Learners compare answers in pairs. Check answers with the class.

> **Answers**
> 1 D 2 B 3 A 4 C

READING FOR DETAIL

3 👤 Pre-teach the word *pulp* [/pʌlp/] (fibres of wood mixed with water until they form a soft wet mass, used for making paper.). Learners read the whole description and find out how these processing stages are carried out in general terms. Warn them that they will be asked to summarize these without looking at the text later, but they can make brief notes under the four headings in this exercise.

4 👥 Learners close their books but can look at their notes. With a partner, they summarize and describe how paper is made. They do not need to give too many details, just show they understand the basic procedure.

> **Answers**
> Obtaining the raw material: the right types of trees are selected
> Processing the raw material: the bark is removed; the wood is cut into small bits, (sometimes it has a chemical removed); it is bleached and cleaned; the pieces are made much smaller.
> Turning raw material into a product: pulp is formed into one object; water is squeezed out, dried and smoothed.
> Making the product ready for market: paper is collected onto rolls

READING BETWEEN THE LINES

5 👤👥 Learners discuss the phrases. Tell them to use their own ideas based on the text and their own knowledge but that they can use a dictionary if they need to. Learners compare answers. Check answers with the class.

> **Possible answers**
> Possible answers:
> 1 the beginning 2 normally 3 better used for/as
> 4 makes better/more useful 5 with the aim/goal of

DISCUSSION

6 👥 👥👥 Learners discuss the questions in pairs or small groups. Give them a few minutes to think about their opinions and language they may need to express them before they start speaking. Monitor to help with vocabulary and to encourage participation. Check a few answers with the class. Encourage learners to respond to each other's ideas.

Answers will vary.

👁 LANGUAGE DEVELOPMENT

ACADEMIC VERB SYNONYMS

1 👤 👥👥 Paraphrase or ask learners to read the information in the box. Ask learners the following questions to check their understanding of the text:

- Do synonyms have exactly the same meaning? (No, not always but they are likely to be very similar.)
- Why should we try to use synonyms in academic writing? (We can make our writing more interesting by avoiding too much repetition. They are also more appropriate to academic writing.)
- Can you think of any dangers of using synonyms? (Synonyms are sometimes used differently, for example, they may use a different preposition or be followed by a different form of a verb than the original word.)

Learners use dictionaries to check meanings of the words where necessary and match them with the synonyms. Point out that these verbs will be useful across a range of academic subjects. Learners compare answers. Check answers with the class.

Answers

1 b 2 a 3 e 4 f 5 g 6 j 7 h 8 i 9 c 10 d

Optional activity (1)

👤 Learners look at a text that they have already studied from their own academic field. They try to find some synonyms in it (not necessarily verbs). They decide whether the words are used in the same way within the sentence.

Optional activity (2)

👥 This game can be played at this stage, after the next activity or later in the unit. Student A looks at Exercise 1 and Student B shuts their books. Student A says a word from either column and the number of letters in the synonym. Student B tries to give the synonym and spell it correctly. They get a point for each correct word. After about five words, learners swap roles.

2 👤 👥👥 Learners read the sentences and complete them with the academic verbs from Exercise 1. Weaker learners can do this in two stages: first they fill in the gaps with words from either column, then they write the academic verb if they have not already done so. Learners compare with a partner. Check answers with the class.

Answers

1 assemble 2 emerge 3 alter 4 enhance 5 cultivate 6 display 7 consult 8 undertake 9 distribute 10 extract

NOMINALIZATION

3 👤 👥👥 Paraphrase or ask learners to read the information in the box. Make sure learners are aware of which highlighted words are noun phrases and which are verb phrases. Point out that if you nominalize a verb you must still have a verb in every sentence. We could rewrite the sentence:

Robots are used to assemble the component parts and glue them together.

as

Robots carry out the assembly and gluing of component parts.

or

The assembly and gluing of component parts is the job of robots.

Learners convert the verb phrases in the exercise into noun phrases. Do at least one example with the whole class. Learners compare answers in pairs. Check answers with the class, showing the words so learners can confirm their spelling. Learners record useful words.

Answers

1 Paper rolling 2 Chocolate distribution 3 Silk creation 4 Production 5 Manufacturing 6 Chocolate consumption

Answers

a alteration b assembly c enhancement d emergence
e distribution f cultivation g display (no change)
h consultation i extraction j undertaking

CRITICAL THINKING

UNDERSTAND

> Give learners a minute to read the writing task they will do at the end of the unit (a description of a process, *Write a description of a process with which you are familiar.*) and keep it in mind as they do the next exercises.

1 👤👥 Learners match the sentences with the pictures. They try to guess unknown vocabulary before checking in dictionaries if necessary. Learners compare with a partner. Check answers with the class.

Answers

1 i 2 g 3 c 4 d 5 j 6 a 7 b 8 e 9 h 10 f

APPLY

2 👤👥 Learners predict the order of the process by writing the stages from Exercise 1 in order. They compare with a partner. Check answers with the class.

Answers

g, a, i, d, f, c, h, e, b, j

WRITING

GRAMMAR FOR WRITING

THE PASSIVE

1 👤👥 Paraphrase or ask learners to read the information in the box. Focus learners on the explanations of the silk manufacturing process on page 97. Ask them what is grammatically different about Sentences 1, 2 and 6 compared to all the others (they are active and the others are passive). Ask why

the writer has used active structures for these particular sentences (because it is important to know who or what did the action – the agent) and why passive constructions have been used for the other sentences (We are interested in the process and not the agent). Now focus on the sentences. Ask learners how we make the passive (the appropriate form of *be* + the past participle or 'third form'). Learners rewrite the sentences to make them passive. Do one or two together with the whole class first. Learners compare answers in pairs. Check answers with the class.

Answers

1 Newspaper is made from hardwood trees.
2 The fabric is made into clothing.
3 Chocolate is eaten at many religious festivals.
4 Silk is considered to be the most luxurious fabric in the world.
5 Patience is needed in the silk manufacturing process.
6 Silk has been produced in China for hundreds of years.
7 The clothes will then be sold for export.

Optional activity 1
As a follow-up, ask learners whether the passive is used mainly in speaking or writing (more in writing, but sometimes in speaking too), in formal or informal language (usually formal). Ask why it is often used in academic writing (it is more formal and less personal, it avoids giving unnecessary information). Learners compare the use of the passive in English with their own language.

2 👤👥 Learners correct the mistakes in the sentences. Point out that these can be related to the passive structure or the verb itself. There may be more than one mistake in each sentence and there is more than one way to correct some of them. Learners compare answers in pairs. Check answers with the class.

Suggested answers

1 Chocolate is made from cocoa beans.
2 Moths lay eggs. / The eggs are laid by moths.
3 The grain is made into flour in a mill.
4 The products are sold in the shops.
5 After the paper is cut, it is stored in large rolls.
6 Once this stage is finished, the silk is sold.
7 Before the process is finished, the chocolate is packaged.
8 Silkworms eat mulberry leaves / Mulberry leaves are eaten by silkworms

SEQUENCING

3 👤👥 Paraphrase or ask learners to read the information in the box. Remind learners that when describing a process the order is important. Draw attention to the tenses used in the example sentences.

Learners rewrite the sentences in Exercise 3. Remind them they have to link the sentences, make them passive and think carefully about the word order and pronouns. Look at the example answer together as a class and do the second sentence together. Learners compare answers in pairs. Check answers with the class.

> **Possible answers**
>
> 2 As soon as they make their cocoons, the silkworms crawl inside.
> 3 Before it is cut into smaller-sized rolls, the paper is collected by a reel.
> 4 Once the beans have been dried, they are transported to chocolate producers around the world.
> 5 Before silkworm eggs were smuggled out of China, only the Chinese could make silk.
> 6 After the fibres are cut to length, oversized particles are removed by the machine.

ACADEMIC WRITING SKILLS

ADDING DETAIL TO YOUR WRITING

1 👥👥 Paraphrase or ask learners to read the information in the box. Learners work in pairs to remember the information to complete the sentences. To make the activity into a game, do not let them look back at the information in the previous sections. Learners exchange their work with another pair and mark each other's answers, now looking back at the unit. They give one point for the correct information and one point if they think the English is correct. At this stage do not tell them if the language is correct or not. They hand the answers back. Check answers with the class. Discuss any different language used by learners.

> **Suggested answers**
>
> 2 for a week 3 along with milk 4 5,000 years ago 5 in her hair 6 which kills the silkworms 7 into small pieces 8 which can be cut into smaller rolls

2 👤👥 Learners reorder the sentences, referring back to the pictures and information on page 97. They compare answers with a partner. Check answers with the class.

> **Answers**
>
> 1 d 2 b 3 c 4 e 5 a

3 👤 Learners turn the information in the previous exercise into a more detailed paragraph. Remind them to use the passive, time phrases, and extra information in their writing. Monitor closely while they are writing to help with any language they need.

> **Suggested answer**
>
> First the moths lay their eggs. After these have hatched, the silkworms are fed mulberry leaves which help them to grow very quickly. Once fully grown, the worms make a cocoon which they then wrap around themselves.

WRITING TASK

WRITING A FIRST DRAFT

1 👤 Focus learners once more on the writing task. Check they understand the title fully by asking the following questions:

- Is this an essay? (No, it is a description of a process.)
- How is a description different from an essay? (You do not give any opinions or extra ideas. You don't need an introduction or a conclusion.)
- What kind of processes could you write about? (How to cook something, play a game, organize a tournament, do something technological or mechanical, succeed at something, write an essay, pass an exam, etc.)
- What should the reader gain from your writing? (An understanding of the different stages of the process.)

If some learners cannot think of a process to describe you could:

- Let them work in groups to brainstorm more ideas.
- Let them share somebody else's idea, although they write alone.

- Print off a process diagram that you think would interest your learners (In a search engine, type '[the process] diagram' and find one that shows a clear progression without too much unknown vocabulary.)

Refer learners back to Reading 2. They should read this quickly once more to get a good idea of what is expected in their writing. They can also refer to other parts of the unit, especially the Critical thinking section. Learners make notes rather than full sentences using the plan provided. Give learners the opportunity to ask you questions about vocabulary or use dictionaries. Tell them they will not be allowed to use dictionaries while they are writing.

2 👤 Learners write the first draft of their description following their plans. Allow about 40 minutes for this. They should write at least 250 words and highlight any language (including spelling) of which they are unsure. Give them a warning five minutes before the end of the set time.

EDIT

3 👤 To encourage learners to take responsibility for their own learning, tell them to check their writing using the task checklist. Stress that this is a very important part of the writing process as it helps learners to learn from their mistakes. Encourage them to look back over their plan and at the unit.

4 👤 Learners make any necessary changes to their description.

5 👤 Learners check their written language now using the language checklist. They can also check any spelling that they were unsure of by looking back over the unit, using a dictionary, or by asking other learners or you. In addition, remind them to check carefully for any errors that they often make in their writing (e.g. particular spellings, subject-verb agreements, omitting verbs, etc.)

6 👤👥 Learners make any other changes and write up their final drafts. If comfortable doing so, they can read each other's writing and suggest improvements before handing the descriptions in to you for marking.

Optional activity

If you have web space for learners' work, the corrected process descriptions could be added. This could be in the style of 'How to' websites such as *wikihow.com* and *howstuffworks.com*.

OBJECTIVES REVIEW

See Introduction, page 9 for ideas about using the Objectives review with your learners.

WORDLIST

See Introduction, page 9 for ideas about how to make the most of the Wordlist with your learners.

REVIEW TEST

See page 107 for the photocopiable Review test for this unit and page 92 for ideas about when and how to administer the Review test.

MODEL ANSWER

See page 129 for the photocopiable Model answer.

RESEARCH PROJECT

Think of a successful local business and research how you would prepare it for the global market.

Divide the class into groups and ask them to think of an important local business, for example a restaurant, a phone company, a clothing or book shop, a construction company or a magazine. Tell the class that this business is going to change from a local business to one suitable for a global market. They should think about what the business will need to change to be suitable for a global market. Each group should think about what the global market wants in comparison to the local market and how the business should change their products, their branding and the way they do business etc. to suit the needs of a global market.

When they have finished their research, each group should write a plan of the changes that the business should make.

ENVIRONMENT

Learning objectives

Focus learners on the Learning objectives box and tell them that this is what they will be working on in this unit. Later they will write a report: *'Write a report which provides both long and short-term solutions to an environmental problem. Refer to a specific case study in your report.'* Show learners this report title on page 119 but reassure them that all the work in this unit will help them to write it. At the end of the unit they will be able to assess how well they can manage the skills in the Learning objectives box.

UNLOCK YOUR KNOWLEDGE

Lead-in

👥 Show the learners the word *weather* written vertically top to bottom in capitals. They have to write words related to weather going across including those letters. Elicit, that the letters *sno* could be written before *w* to make the word *snow* and that the capital letter can be anywhere in the word. Learners work in pairs to try to complete the other six words.

Possible answers

snoW
hurricanE
rAin
droughT
Hail
tEmperature
thundeR

👥 Learners discuss the three questions in pairs. Monitor to help with vocabulary, and encourage participation. Check some answers with the class. Check understanding of vocabulary in the questions by asking the following questions:

- Which word means there's so much water that it gets into people's houses?(flood /flʌd/)
- Which word has the opposite meaning? (drought /draʊt/), meaning there is not enough rain)
- What word could replace impact? (effect) Which word has a stronger meaning? (impact)

Possible answers

1 Floods: excess rainfall / water and poor defences. Drought: excess heat / lack of rain. Impact of floods: loss of life by drowning, damaged buildings and possessions, homelessness, loss of crops, animals,

jobs, etc. Impact of drought: starvation, loss of crops and animals, lack of water for hygiene and drinking can cause disease.
2 Storms, earthquakes, sand storms, tornados, tsunamis, disease epidemics, famine. Impact of these natural disasters can include loss of life, damaged buildings and possessions, homelessness, loss of crops, animals, jobs, etc. starvation, lack of water for hygiene and drinking.

WATCH AND LISTEN

Video script

THE THREE GORGES DAM

The Yangtze river in China is the world's third longest river. It is beautiful, with a rich history. As a major trade route it provides jobs for many people who live along it. However, the river is unpredictable and in the past has often flooded, resulting in the death and homelessness of many local people. In 1998, there was a particularly bad flood when 300 million people were displaced.

The Chinese government had already decided to control the floods by building a dam. Construction of the Three Gorges Dam began in 1994. Completed in 2008, the dam controls the flow of water in the Yangtze and protects the inhabitants in the area below it from flooding.

One additional advantage is that it now provides cheap, clean electricity through the world's biggest hydroelectric power station built into the dam. It provides 10% of China's electricity.

One of the disadvantages is, is that in order to achieve the building of the dam, much of the surrounding area behind the dam needed to be submerged. This meant the loss of 13 cities and numerous towns and villages with the relocation of 2 million people. Thousands of years of cultural heritage in the form of ancient buildings were also lost.

This extraordinary engineering project is an example of what can be achieved with sufficient planning and vision. The dam has resulted in increased security for inhabitants living along the river and provided an additional source of much needed energy, but this has not been without a cost.

PREPARING TO WATCH

USING YOUR KNOWLEDGE TO PREDICT CONTENT

1 👥 Focus learners on the photos of the dam and elicit what it is. Learners discuss the questions, using the photographs to help them with ideas. Check learners' ideas with the class, but do not give any answers yet. Tell them they will hear the answers to the questions soon.

2 👥 Focus learners on the photographs. They discuss in pairs what each one shows and what they think the presenter will say about each picture. Again, listen to some ideas but do not give any answers yet.

3 👥 Learners watch the video and then discuss with their partner which of their predictions were correct.

4 👥 Learners use the explanation box to work out the definitions of the words. They can use a dictionary to check their answers

> **Answers**
>
> 1 under water 2 not possible 3 not predictable
> 4 special 5 move to a new place 6 not an advantage

UNDERSTANDING KEY VOCABULARY

5 👥 Remind learners or elicit from them that collocations are pairs of words that go together with a specific meaning. In this exercise they will look at one word and find two others that can be used with it to make collocations. Focus learners on the example. Point out that *rich* has a different meaning depending which word it is with. Learners continue the exercise in pairs. Check answers with the class.

> **Answers**
>
> 1 b, c 2 a, c 3 b, c 4 a, b (*cultural heritage* means features belonging to the culture of a particular society, such as traditions, languages, or buildings, that were created in the past and still have historical importance) 5 a, b 6 b, c 7 a, c

WHILE WATCHING

LISTENING FOR KEY INFORMATION

6 ▶ 👤👥 Tell learners they are going to watch the video again. First, they look at the statements about the Three Gorges Dam

and complete the sentences with the missing words. Learners watch the video to check their answers. They compare answers. Check answers with the class.

> **Answers**
>
> 1 jobs 2 homelessness 3 Chinese government
> 4 inhabitants 5 power station 6 ancient 7 vision

UNDERSTANDING DETAIL

7 ▶ 👤👥 Learners read the sentences and try to fill them with the figures from the box, by remembering or guessing the answers. They compare answers and watch the video again to check. Check answers with the class.

> **Answers**
>
> 1 3rd 2 300 3 10% 4 13 5 2

RESPONDING TO THE VIDEO CONTENT

8 👥 Learners discuss the questions in pairs. Monitor to help with vocabulary and to encourage participation. Check a few answers with the class. Encourage learners to respond to each other's ideas.

> **Answers**
>
> 1 Overall it is quite neutral, perhaps with a slight bias towards being positive (especially at the end of the video).
> 2 This is a sensitive issue, and learners may have many different opinions. Some feel that economic development is the most important focus for a country, whereas others think that cultural preservation is of more importance. Submerging large areas of land underwater is obviously very disruptive for local communities.

DISCUSSION

9 👥 👥👥 Learners discuss the questions in pairs or small groups. Give them a few minutes to think about their opinions and any language they may need to express them before they start speaking. Monitor to help with vocabulary and to encourage participation. Check a few answers with the class. Encourage learners to respond to each other's ideas.

> **Answers will vary**

READING 1

PREPARING TO READ

UNDERSTANDING KEY VOCABULARY

1 👤👥 Focus learners on the photographs and ask them what they think the topic of the reading will be (*flooding*). Ask if they know what any of the pictures show (in English). Learners look at the words in the box and match them to the pictures, using dictionaries if necessary. Learners compare answers. Check answers with the class. When checking, establish which answers are natural events (*tsunami* and *hurricane*) and which are types of protection (*levee, dam, flood barrier, sandbagging*). Use the notes below to help clarify vocabulary if necessary.

Answers

1 levee: a wall made of land or other materials that is built next to a river to stop it from overflowing
2 dam: a wall built across a river which stops its flow and collects the water, usually to make a reservoir (= an artificial lake) which provides water for an area
3 flood barrier: a type of gate on a river that can be closed to stop water flooding an area
4 tsunami: an extremely large wave caused by movement of the Earth under the sea, often caused by an earthquake
5 hurricane: a violent wind which has a circular movement
6 sandbagging: protection against flooding using bags filled with sand

2 👤👥 Give learners two or three minutes to skim read the interview and decide which is the best title. If they ask you what *disaster mitigation* means, tell them that it will be explained in the interview. Learners compare with a partner, justifying their answer. Check answers with the class.

Answers

1 *Controlling the flow is the best title* because the interview is about ways to control the flow of water in a flood.
2 is not as good because the interviewer does not suggest a best way to protect flooding and also says people also have to help themselves in a flood situation.

3 is not as good because it is too general and does not mention water or flooding.
4 is not as good because the text is not just about protecting houses.

WHILE READING

READING FOR DETAIL

3 👤👥 Focus learners on the statements and remind them of the difference between *false* and *does not say*. Do one or two examples with the whole class, eliciting the reasons for the answers in the text. Learners compare answers, saying what is wrong with the false statements. Check answers with the class.

Answers

1 F (He works for a government ministry.) 2 T
3 DNS 4 F (They cannot withstand the power of a tsunami.) 5 T 6 T 7 DNS 8 T

4 👤👥 Paraphrase or ask learners to read the information in the box. Point out the words and phrases in bold in the text and tell learners they have to find the nouns or noun phrases they refer to in the text. Do the first example together. With a weaker group, do one or more examples with the whole class. They complete the exercise. Learners compare answers in pairs. If they have different answers, encourage them to justify why.

Answers

1 risk reduction and risk analysis
2 risk reduction
3 earth wall defences or levees
4 the case of a tsunami
5 the government ministry
6 flood prevention solutions
7 the Thames barrier
8 expensive early warning systems

Optional activity

Learners can do a similar activity to the one above with any text. Encourage them to take a text from their own field of study, highlight the pronouns and nouns (such as *case, measures, areas*) and work out what they refer to.

READING BETWEEN THE LINES

MAKING INFERENCES FROM THE TEXT

5 👥👥 Learners read the statements about flood control, discuss which ones they think Dan Smith would agree with and tick them. Point out that the answers are not in the text, so they will need to infer them. They compare answers with another pair. Check answers with the class.

DISCUSSION

6 👥 👥👥 Learners discuss the questions. Point out that Question 1 is hypothetical so learners will need conditional structures to answer it. Monitor to help with vocabulary and to encourage participation. Check a few answers with the class. Encourage learners to respond to each other's ideas.

Answers

1 and 2 Answers may vary.
3 Bangladesh, China, India, Pakistan. Heavy monsoon rains and global warming means snow and ice on the Himalayas is melting into rivers and increasing the risk of flooding in these countries.

READING 2

Optional lead-in

👥👥👥 There are several country names in this unit so it is worth spending some time on the spelling of these. Learners work in groups of about four. They think of as many countries as they can ending in a letter or group of letters you give them in one minute (longer for weaker groups). One person writes and the others suggest countries. They should not look up the answers at this stage. Ask questions such as the following: (Possible answers are given, although there are many more.)

- Which countries end with *-land*? (*England, Ireland, Thailand, Poland, Switzerland, Finland, Iceland*)
- Which countries end with the letter *a*? (*China, Kenya, Saudi Arabia, Algeria, Argentina, Canada, Bosnia, Botswana, Indonesia, India, Romania*)
- Which countries end with the letter *n*? (*Jordan, Afghanistan, Oman, Sudan, Japan, Spain, Pakistan, Kazakhstan*)

Check answers orally. Each group gets one point for each country they get right and one extra point for each correctly spelled country.

PREPARING TO READ

USING YOUR KNOWLEDGE TO PREDICT CONTENT

1 👥👥👥 Introduce the subject of drought. Focus learners on the map and establish what it shows (the average air temperature around the world in December). Learners discuss where they think the most common areas of drought are and why. If they do not know the names of countries, they can point or refer to a world map on which countries are named. Check answers with the class.

Answers

1 Droughts are most common in countries which have little rain. These are predominantly found in sub-Saharan Africa. Australia also suffers badly, but as a richer country is better able to mitigate the problems arising from little or no rain. On the map, the areas with the highest temperatures (in red) and little rainfall are the most likely ones to suffer from drought: Africa and Australia.
2 and 3 Answers will vary.

2 👥👥 Learners discuss the questions. Tell them that this will help them to understand the text they are going to read which deals with the same questions. Check the meaning of *struggle* (find something difficult). Monitor to help with vocabulary and to encourage participation. Check a few ideas with the class, but do not give any answers at this stage.

Answers

1 Drought kills animals and crops and causes starvation.
2 Bottles of drinking water can be brought into the drought area.
3 Drought monitoring, rainwater harvesting and water recycling.
4 Many long-term drought solutions are expensive and need technical knowledge which may not be available.

WHILE READING

READING FOR MAIN IDEAS

3 👤 👥👥 Learners read the six purposes and match them with the paragraphs in the text. Give them no more than one minute to look at the essay and do this. Check the meaning of *brief*

(purpose f, give somebody information they may need). Learners compare with a partner. Check answers with the class.

Answers

a 6 b 5 c 1 d 4 e 3 f 2

READING FOR DETAIL

4 Focus learners' attention on the diagram. If learners have not seen this kind of graphic organizer (a four-quadrant graph) before, spend some time familiarizing them with the concept. The more long-term a solution is, the further to the right it should be, and the more expensive it is, the higher it should be, etc. Strategy number 1 is long-term and expensive, so it should go in the top right of the graph. Do the next one or two as a class before learners complete the graph if you feel they are struggling. Learners plot the rest of the ideas on the graph. They compare with a partner. Check answers with the class. Learners may have plotted the solutions in slightly different places. If they are very different, ask them to justify their answers.

Possible answers

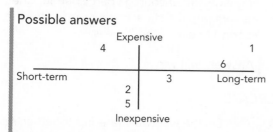

READING BETWEEN THE LINES

INFERRING MEANING

5 Learners read the multiple-choice questions and come to their own conclusions before discussing with a partner. Check answers with the class.

Answers

1 c 2 c 3 b

DISCUSSION

6 Learners discuss the questions in pairs or small groups. Give them a few minutes to think about their opinions and language they may need to express them before they

start speaking. Check the meaning of the word *severe* /sɪˈvɪər/ in this context (serious, extreme). Monitor to help with vocabulary and to encourage participation. Check a few answers with the class. Encourage learners to respond to each other's ideas.

Answers will vary.

⊙ LANGUAGE DEVELOPMENT

ACADEMIC NOUN PHRASES

1 Paraphrase or ask learners to read the information in the box and remind them of the work they did on nominalization in Unit 5. Learners rewrite the sentences. Do one or two together with the class as examples. Note that the noun phrase may consist of two or three words. Learners compare answers. Check answers with the class. Learners record useful words.

Answers

1 disaster mitigation 2 risk reduction 3 water management system 4 government report 5 flood protection 6 community projects

NATURAL DISASTERS

2 Remind learners that collocations are words that are used together with a particular meaning. Point out all three adjectives make good collocations with the noun but that two of the adjectives have a similar meaning and one has a different meaning. Look at the first one with the class. *Natural disasters* refers to the type of disaster (hurricanes, floods, droughts, etc.) while the other two refer to the scale or impact of it. Learners work in pairs, using a dictionary if necessary. Model and drill *severe*, *devastating* /ˈdev.ə.steɪ.tɪŋ/ and *ambitious* /æmˈbɪʃ.əs/. Check answers with the class. Learners record useful words.

Answers

1 natural (Examples of natural disasters are hurricanes, floods, droughts etc. *catastrophic* and *major* both talk about the extent and impact of a disaster.)
2 controlled (This means a flood which is pre-planned, for example by allowing some water to pass through a dam. *Severe* and *devastating* both refer to the extent and impact of a flood.)

> 3 long-term (This means that the project will take a long time to complete. *Ambitious* and *large-scale* refer to the size of the project.)
> 4 seasonal (This means that the drought happens at the same time each year. *Prolonged* and *extreme* suggest a longer period of time with worse effects.)

3 👤👥 Learners use collocations from the previous exercise to complete the sentences. Point out that they may need to make them plural. Some sentences have more than one correct answer. Do the first one together. Ask which of the four nouns (*disaster, project, flood* or *drought*) to use (*project*). Singular or plural? (*plants* tells us that it must be plural) Ask which adjective describes *take many years to construct* (*long-term*). Learners compare with a partner. Check answers with the class.

> **Possible answers**
>
> 1 long-term projects 2 natural disasters 3 controlled floods 4 ambitious / large-scale projects 5 devastating / severe flood 6 extreme drought 7 seasonal drought 8 catastrophic / major disaster

CRITICAL THINKING

> Give learners a minute to read the writing task they will do at the end of the unit (a report, *Write a report which provides both long and short-term solutions to an environmental problem. Refer to a specific case study in your report.*) and keep it in mind as they do the next exercises.

ANALYZE

1 👤 Check the meaning of *case study* (information focused on one particular example of something, especially in order to show general principles). Tell learners that this section of the unit will be very useful, as it will provide them with case studies to base their reports on. Learners read through the case studies and strategies. They may need help with the following vocabulary:

- *GDP rank*: Gross domestic product (GDP) is the total value of all goods and services produced in an economy. A country's GDP ranking shows how rich it is in comparison to other countries, for example, Australia is the twelfth richest country in the world.
- *Habitat*: a natural environment where an animal lives.
- *Tectonic plates*: sections of the planet's surface.
- *Reinforced*: made stronger.

- *Infrastructure*: the basic systems and services, such as transport and power supplies, that a country or organization uses in order to work effectively.
- *Deforestation*: the cutting down of trees in a large area, or the destruction of forests by people.
- *Fertile*: describes land that can produce a large number of good quality crops.
- *Visibility*: how far you can see clearly.

Learners decide which strategies apply to which case study. Each case study may have more than one possible strategy and each strategy may apply to more than one case study. Reassure learners that they do not need to know the answers here, but they should be able to give a reason for their choices.

> **Possible answers**
>
> 1 – C; 2 – A, B, C, D; 3 – A, B, D; 4 – A, D; 5 – D; 6 – C; 7 – A, B, C, D; 8 – A, B, C, D

2 👥 Learners discuss the strategies in relation to the problems in the case studies, justifying their answers and saying how they would help in each situation. Monitor to help with language and encourage participation. Check answers with the class. Encourage learners to respond to each other's ideas.

> **Answers will vary.**

CREATE

3 👥👥 Do the first two strategies together. Ask learners to assess whether replanting suitable trees would be expensive (medium cost) and whether it would be a short or long-term solution (long term). Learners write number 1 on the appropriate part of the chart. Do the same with strategy 2. Learners continue the task in pairs. This should generate plenty of discussion. Monitor to help with language, understanding and participation. Learners compare their chart with another pair. Check answers with the class. Learners' charts may look very different but that is not a problem as long as they can justify their answers.

> **Possible answers**

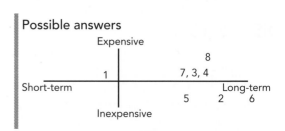

WRITING

GRAMMAR FOR WRITING

EXPRESSING SOLUTIONS USING *IT*

1 🧍👥 Focus learners on the sentence in Question 3 of the Academic noun phrases exercise on page 114: *It is important for a country to have a system for managing water to protect against flooding.* Ask what *It* refers to in this sentence. The answer is nothing! Sometimes we use *it* as an 'empty' pronoun (one without any meaning) because we need a subject to make a sentence grammatically correct. This may be a difficult concept for learners to understand, but should become clear through this activity.

Paraphrase or ask learners to read the information in the box. Learners read the beginnings and ends of the sentences and match them. Stress again that *it* has no meaning, but that these are useful phrases for them to learn for their academic writing. They need to consider the grammatical structures that follow various *it* phrases, but also the best overall meaning of the sentence. For this they need to remember or refer back to the information they have read. Learners compare with a partner. Check answers with the class.

> **Possible answers**
> 1 b 2 f 3 c 4 a 5 h 6 e 7 d 8 g

2 🧍👥👥 Learners complete the sentences with their own ideas. Weaker learners may need to work in pairs. Monitor to help with language and refer learners back to the reading texts if they have no ideas or are unsure about vocabulary and spelling. Learners compare with a partner (or with another pair). Check answers with the class.

> **Possible answers**
> 1 ...using sandbags to stop water.
> 2 ...on high ground.
> 3 ...harvesting and storing rainwater.
> 4 ...to get people to agree on a strategy.
> 5 ...that they are expensive.
> 6 ...crucial that people take notice of it.

> **Optional activity**
>
> Learners look at a report from their own field of study and either find examples of these types of *it* phrases, or write some of their own based on information given in a report they have chosen.

ACADEMIC WRITING SKILLS

PARAGRAPH STRUCTURE IN ESSAYS

1 🧍👥 It is important that learners know about the form and function of paragraphs in academic essays in English, especially if it is different from their native language. They read the sentences and tick the ones that are true. They also think about why the others are wrong. Learners compare with a partner. Check answers with the class.

> **Answers**
> True: 2, 3, 4 and 6
> False:
> 1 A text broken into paragraphs may look better, but this is not the main reason for writing them.
> 5 No, points in a paragraph should go from general to specific.
> 7 A paragraph should generally contain more than two sentences, but there is no set number.

Learners read the information in the box. Point out that paragraph structures are not only for essays but also apply to reports and other academic writing. There are different structures that learners are likely to read but it is a good idea for them to start writing their paragraphs like this.

2 🧍👥 Learners read the five sentences and reorder them to make a coherent paragraph which follows the plan in the box. They compare with a partner. Check answers with the class.

> **Answers**
> 1 b 2 c 3 e 4 a 5 d

3 🧍👥 Learners use the model above to write a paragraph about protecting a house from a flood. Before they start writing, brainstorm some ideas they can use in the paragraph. Use these prompts if necessary: *sandbags*; *move furniture*; *move possessions*; *move* *residents (especially children, the sick and the elderly); help neighbours.* Learners follow the three stages given. Monitor to give language and content help where needed. Learners compare with a partner and help each other to improve their paragraphs. Check answers with the class.

Answers

Model paragraph

There are several measures householders can take to protect their house from a flood. It will probably be impossible to keep all water out of the house but the following steps will help to minimize water damage and keep people safe. Firstly, the residents need to decide whether they should stay in the house or not, depending on the severity of the flood and the age and health of the occupants. Next as many items of furniture and other possessions as possible should be moved upstairs. Finally, sandbags should be piled outside doors to prevent too much water entering the house.

WRITING TASK

PLAN

1 👤 Focus learners once more on the writing task. Check they understand the title fully by asking the following questions:

- Is it an essay? (No, it's a report.)
- Do you write about different types of environmental problems? (No, just one.)
- Should you focus mainly on short-term or long-term solutions? (Aim for a balance between the two.)
- Where will you find case study information? (In the *Critical thinking* section, or you can write about your own country or another you know well.)
- Should you make recommendations? (Yes, a report usually includes recommendations. In this case make them for your case study.)

Learners look back over the unit and chose an environmental problem from the Critical thinking section or one they know about and make notes, rather than full sentences, using the plan provided. Give learners the opportunity to ask you questions about vocabulary or use dictionaries. Tell them they will not be allowed to use dictionaries while they are writing.

WRITING A FIRST DRAFT

2 👤 Learners write the first draft of their report following their plans. Allow about 40 minutes for this. They should write at least 250 words

and highlight any language (including spelling) of which they are unsure. Give them a warning five minutes before the end of the set time.

EDIT

3–6 👤 To encourage learners to take responsibility for their own learning, tell them to check their writing using the task checklist. Stress that this is a very important part of the writing process as it helps learners to learn from their mistakes. Encourage them to look back over their plan and at the unit.

OBJECTIVES REVIEW

See Introduction, page 9 for ideas about using the Objectives review with your learners.

WORDLIST

See Introduction, page 9 for ideas about how to make the most of the Wordlist with your learners.

REVIEW TEST

See page 110 for the photocopiable Review test for this unit and page 92 for ideas about when and how to administer the Review test.

MODEL ANSWER

See page 130 for the photocopiable Model answer.

RESEARCH PROJECT

Calculate your environmental impact and take measures to reduce it.

This initially is an individual project. Tell the class that they will calculate their environmental impact. Learners should think about how much and how they travel, flights they have taken, the size of their house and how much energy it uses, whether they recycle or not and their diet. They could use an online calculator to help them.

They can then compare their impact, in groups, and make a graphical representation of this compared to the country as a whole, and other countries.

They can then formulate their own class pledge to reduce their impact, sign this and then try and market this idea to others.

7 ARCHITECTURE

Learning objectives

Focus learners on the Learning objectives box and tell them that this is what they will be working on in this unit. Later they will write an essay: 'Which is more important when building a new home: its location or its size?' Show learners this essay title on page 138 but reassure them that all the work in this unit will help them to write it. At the end of the unit they will be able to assess how well they can manage the skills in the Learning objectives box.

UNLOCK YOUR KNOWLEDGE

Lead-in (1)

Before the lesson sketch out the floor plan of your home. Do not show learners, but describe it to them and ask them to draw it. Show them your plan when they have finished so they can compare. Learners now sketch the floor plan of their own home or another house they know. Allow only two minutes for this – assure them it does not need to be very accurate or neat. Learners then describe their floor plan to a partner, who has to draw it. They work in pairs, describing and drawing. Monitor to help with language and note level of ability to talk about buildings. At the end of the activity, learners compare their drawings with the originals.

Lead-in (2)

This activity is shorter than Lead-in 1. Learners look at a photo of a city skyline and in pairs say in what ways it is similar to and different from the skyline of their own town or city. Monitor to help with language and guide learners to talk about any architectural features. Check answers with the class.

Learners discuss the questions in pairs or small groups. Monitor to help with vocabulary, encourage participation and check learners' level of existing knowledge on the topic. Check some ideas with the class.

Answers will vary.

WATCH AND LISTEN

Video script

ISLAMIC ARCHITECTURE

Islamic architecture has been built in a wide range of styles from the foundation of Islam to the present day. The main Islamic architectural types are: the palace, the mosque and the tomb.

One of the greatest Islamic palaces is the Alhambra in Spain. Alhambra means 'the red one' in Arabic. It was built during the 14th century by the rulers of the Emirate of Granada. These days it is a popular tourist destination.

The buildings were designed to reflect the beauty of paradise. The extensive gardens, for which a special irrigation system was built, contain many fountains and pools. And water channels inside the buildings themselves acted as air conditioning, helping to keep the rooms in the Alhambra cool.

The magnificent decoration consists of leaves and trees, Arabic writing, and beautiful delicate patterns. And yet from the outside, the building simply looks like a fortress, with 13 huge impressive towers.

Islamic architecture is also famous for religious buildings.

The Sultan Ahmed Mosque is a historical mosque in Istanbul, the largest city in Turkey. The mosque is known as the Blue Mosque for the blue tiles which cover the inside walls. It was built between 1609 and 1616, during the rule of Ahmed I. The writing on the walls is originally by the great 17th century calligrapher Ametli Kasim Gubarim.

A heavy iron chain hangs in the entrance on the western side. The chain was put there so that the sultan, who rode in on a horse, had to lower his head to enter the mosque.

Perhaps the finest example of Islamic tomb architecture is the Taj Mahal in India. It was built by Mughal emperor Shah Jahan in memory of his wife. The building is covered with designs in paint, carved marble and precious stones.

It was constructed using materials from India, China, Afghanistan and the gulf of Arabia. The architects came from Turkey, Iran and Pakistan and it was built by 10,000 Indian workers. The Taj Mahal perfectly demonstrates how the ideas of Islamic architecture spread around the world.

PREPARING TO WATCH

USING YOUR KNOWLEDGE TO PREDICT CONTENT

1 Focus learners on the three photographs. Ask if they can match them with the names of the buildings. They compare answers with a partner. Check answers with the class. Find out if learners know anything else about these buildings and whether anybody in the class has visited them.

> Answers
> 1 c 2 b 3 a

UNDERSTANDING KEY VOCABULARY

2 Learners match the words to the definitions using a dictionary if necessary. Learners compare answers with a partner. Check answers with the class. Model and drill vocabulary as necessary.

> Answers
> 1 e 2 f 3 b 4 i 5 d 6 a 7 h 8 j 9 c 10 g

Optional activity

To help learners notice spelling, ask these questions:

Which word has a silent letter? (*tomb*) Can you think of any other words that end with m + silent b? (*bomb, comb, lamb, climb, thumb* etc.)

- Which words include the sound /k/? Notice how they are spelled. (*mosque, architect*) Can you think of any more words that end in -*que* (pronounced /k/)? (*unique, antique, technique, boutique, cheque* etc.) Can you think of any more words that have a /k/ sound, spelted *ch*? (*school, chemist, ache, stomach* etc.) The words ending in -*que* come from French and the words with *ch* as a /k/ sound are of Greek origin.

- Look at the word *empire* and *emperor*. What do you notice about the spelling? (They have different vowels after the *p*. This is irregular and unusual.) Can you think of any other jobs or positions that end in *or*? (*actor, ambassador, contractor, director, doctor, instructor, professor, solicitor* etc.)

Learners record any useful words.

WHILE WATCHING

UNDERSTANDING MAIN IDEAS

3 Tell learners that they are going to watch a video about the three buildings shown in the photos in Exercise 1. While they are watching they think about the questions. If your learners are all from Islamic countries, they could discuss Question 1 (or all three if they know the three buildings) before watching. Learners watch the video and compare answers with a partner. Check some ideas with the class.

> Possible answers
> 1 Some adjectives they may use (but of course there are many others): *decorative, beautiful, ornate, delicate, airy.*
> 2 and 3 Answers will vary.

LISTENING FOR KEY INFORMATION

4 Learners look at the table and predict or try to remember the missing words before they watch the video again. Check the meaning of *features* (typical qualities or important parts of something) and *precious* (rare, expensive or important). Learners watch the video to check their answers, checking the spelling of the words they have written by referring to the previous exercise or a dictionary if necessary. They compare answers. Check answers with the class.

> Answers
> 1 palace 2 gardens 3 building 4 blue 5 writing 6 tomb 7 stones 8 architects

5 Learners read the list of details and write the building (a, b or c) next to each one. They watch the video again to check.

Check the meaning and pronunciation of iron /aɪən/ (a strong silver-coloured metal used for making steel) and calligraphy /kəˈlɪg.rə.fi/ (beautiful writing, often produced with a pen or brush). Learners compare answers. Check answers with the class.

| Answers

1 c 2 a 3 b 4 b 5 a 6 c 7 b 8 b 9 a

DISCUSSION

6 👥 👥👥 Learners discuss the questions in pairs or small groups. Give them a few minutes to think about their opinions and any language they may need to express them before they start speaking. Monitor to help with vocabulary and to encourage participation. Check a few answers with the class. Encourage learners to respond to each other's ideas.

| Answers will vary.

READING 1

PREPARING TO READ

USING YOUR KNOWLEDGE TO PREDICT CONTENT

1 👥 👥👥 Focus learners on the photograph and ask how they would feel about living there. Learners discuss the questions in pairs. Monitor to help with language and encourage participation. Learners compare answers with another pair. Check ideas with the class but do not give any answers at the moment as these will be answered in the reading later.

UNDERSTANDING KEY VOCABULARY

2 👤 👥 Learners complete the sentences with the given words using a dictionary if necessary. Learners compare answers with a partner. Check answers with the class.

| Answers

1 durable 2 efficiency 3 straw/mud (or mud/straw)
4 compromise 5 install 6 green 7 solar panels
8 affordable

WHILE READING

SKIMMING

3 👤 Paraphrase or ask learners to read the information in the box. Ask learners which other situations they may find themselves in where they need to skim read (exams, choosing whether to read something or not in the library, reading the newspaper etc.) In order to answer the first multiple-choice question, learners should not read the whole article, just look at the title, introduction, conclusion and illustrations.

| Answer

d

4 👥 Learners compare their answers to Exercise 1 and discuss which part of the text helped them to reach that answer.

5 👤 👥 Focus learners on the ideas. Check vocabulary by asking for two ways to say environmentally-friendly (green and the prefix eco-). They skim read the article to match the ideas with the paragraphs. Give a maximum of three minutes for this to discourage learners from reading each word in the text. Learners compare answers in pairs. Check answers with the class.

| Answers

a 2 b 3 c 1 d 5 e 4

READING FOR DETAIL

6 👤 Focus learners on the architectural features. Do the first feature together. Ask learners whether the grass roof belongs to Howe Dell school, the Hobbit House or neither. Learners complete the exercise alone. They compare answers with a partner. Check answers with the class.

| Answers

1 HH 2 HH 3 N 4 HH 5 HD 6 N (the school makes furniture out of old materials, but it doesn't say the furniture is second-hand) 7 HH 8 HD 9 HH 10 HH

7 👤 👥 Learners read the statements and decide if they are true, false or it does not say. They complete the exercise. Learners compare answers, saying what is wrong with the false statements. Check answers with the class.

Answers

1 T 2 DNS 3 F (It remains to be seen whether customers will pay more in the future.) 4 T 5 T 6 F (They are non-renewable.) 7 DNS 8 T

READING BETWEEN THE LINES

MAKING INFERENCES FROM THE TEXT

8 Learners discuss the questions, referring back to the text if necessary. Remind them that when they make inferences, the exact answer may not be in the text and they need to use their own knowledge to work out the answers. Learners compare answers with another pair. Check answers with the class.

Suggested answers

1 There is more awareness about global warming.
2 Learners probably learn about the importance of natural resources, and respect for the environment.
3 Some countries, like the UK, cannot realistically produce much energy from solar panels because of the lack of sunlight.
4 Many people like to support environmentally-friendly companies to seem 'green', especially if it does not cost them any more money.

DISCUSSION

9 Learners discuss the questions. Point out that Question 1 is hypothetical so learners will need conditional structures to answer it. Monitor to help with vocabulary and to encourage participation. Check a few answers with the class. Encourage learners to respond to each other's ideas.

Answers will vary.

READING 2

PREPARING TO READ

USING YOUR KNOWLEDGE TO PREDICT CONTENT

1 Learners read the questions. Allow them some time to think about their answers alone. They then discuss their responses in pairs. Monitor to help with language and encourage participation. Check ideas with the class. Encourage learners to respond to each other's ideas.

2 Learners skim read the text and find out the author's opinion of whether beauty or functionality is more important. Discourage dictionary use at this stage and set a time limit of two or three minutes to look at the text so they do not read every word. Learners compare with a partner. Check answers with the class.

Answers

The writer thinks beauty and function are equally important in creating perfect architecture.

WHILE READING

READING FOR MAIN IDEAS

3 Learners read the summary and fill in any gaps they already know or can guess with one or two words. They then refer back to the text to complete the other gaps, checking spelling carefully. Learners compare with a partner. Check answers with the class.

Answers

1 function 2 beauty 3 architects 4 building 5 users 6 mood/happiness 7 reflect 8 Blending 9 celebrated

4 Learners read the original sentences and the paraphrases (remind them that this means the same information given in different words) and match them. They compare with a partner. Check answers with the class.

Answers

1 b 2 a 3 f 4 c 5 e 6 d

READING BETWEEN THE LINES

MAKING INFERENCES FROM THE TEXT

5 Learners read the questions and come to their own conclusions before discussing their ideas with a partner. Point out that the answers are not in the text, so they will need their own knowledge to answer them. Check answers with the class.

Possible answers

1 They can create a more positive and inspired workforce. They allow the users of the building to function well. They can give a positive impression of the owner to other people.

2 It maximizes the number of planes which can fit in the airport.

3 In case the buildings reflect badly on them.

4 The lighting, lack of or poor view from windows, the temperature inside the building (either too cold or too hot), decoration.

5 If workers have been provided with a comfortable and pleasant working environment they may feel more appreciated and want to work harder for the company.

DISCUSSION

6 👥 👥👥 Learners discuss the questions in pairs or small groups. Give them a few minutes to think about their opinions and language they may need to express them before they start speaking. Check that they understand the phrase *if money were no object* (it doesn't matter how much it costs, because you are very rich and can afford whatever you want!) Monitor to help with vocabulary and to encourage participation. Check a few answers with the class. Encourage learners to respond to each other's ideas.

| Answers will vary.

⦿ LANGUAGE DEVELOPMENT

ACADEMIC WORD FAMILIES

1 👤👥 Paraphrase or ask learners to read the information in the box. Ask the following questions to check understanding:

- How do we usually make different words in one family? (By adding suffixes to the base form or changing suffixes to change the word class.)
- What about prefixes? (These do not change the class of a word but do change the meaning, such as positive to negative.)
- Is the base form in a word family always a complete word? (No. Sometimes the base form only makes a complete word when it is used with a suffix, e.g. if you take the *-ment* suffix off *environment* we are left with *environ*, which is not a word in itself.)

Focus learners on the words in the table. Ask them to highlight the suffixes used here for nouns (*-ion*, *-ism*, *-ment*, *-ibility*), for adjectives (*-al*, *-ing*) and adverbs (*ly*). Point out that there

are others too, although *ly* is by far the most common suffix for adverbs.

Focus on the word family for *function* and help learners see how the other members of the word family are built up. Point out that a dark space in the table means that there is no word from the same family for this word class. Learners try to work out what the words could be and then check in a dictionary if necessary. Early finishers can write example sentences using the different words. Learners compare answers. Check answers with the class. Learners record useful words.

Answers

1 environmental 2 environmentally 3 depression
4 depress 5 depressingly 6 responsible 7 responsibly
8 architecture 9 architectural 10 architecturally
11 efficiency 12 efficient

Optional activity

👤 As well as learning some typical suffixes for different word classes (part of speech), it is helpful for learners to know how these are added to base words. There are some reasonably regular patterns to help them:

- A suffix is usually added to the whole base word: *efficient + -ly = efficiently*. The same principle applies if there is more than one suffix: *environment + -al +-ly = environmentally*.
- Some suffixes begin with a vowel (vowel suffixes) and some begin with a consonant (consonant suffixes). If the base word ends with a silent *e*, like *use* or *state*, we usually keep that *e* before a consonant suffix (*use + -ful = useful, state + -ment = statement*). However, if a word ending with silent *e* is followed by a vowel suffix, we usually drop the *e* (*use + -ual = usual, value + -able = valuable, state + -ing = stating*).
- Base words that end in *-ce* or *-ge* often keep the *e* before a suffix that begins with *a, o* or *u* (to keep the 'soft' /s/ and /dʒ/ (g) pronunciation), for example *manageable* and *noticeable*.
- Base words that end in consonant + *y* change the *y* to an *i* before any suffixes that do not begin with *i* themselves (*friendly + -ness = friendliness, study + -ing = studying*). If there is a vowel before the *y*, there is no change (*enjoy + -ment = enjoyment*).
- As explored in Unit 6, a final consonant before a vowel suffix is usually doubled if the base word ends in a stressed consonant-vowel-consonant pattern (*running, inferring*). Note, however, that some letters do not usually double in English (except across two parts of a compound word), such as *h, j, k, q, w, x* and *y* (*renew + -able = renewable, pay + -ing = paying*).

Teach these points according to learners' needs, considering errors that you have noticed in their writing. Learners keep records of useful words and examples. They could also look at some academic writing from their own field of study and find more examples of words with suffixes related to their own subject. They keep records of these.

2 Learners complete the sentences with words from the previous exercise. Encourage them to check the spelling carefully. They compare answers with a partner. Check answers with the class.

> **Answers**
>
> 1 environmental 2 Functionalizm 3 efficient
> 4 responsibly 5 depress 6 architecture
> 7 environment 8 responsible 9 depression
> 10 architectural

ARCHITECTURE AND PLANNING

3 Learners complete the definitions using a dictionary if necessary. Learners compare answers with a partner. Check answers with the class.

> **Answers**
>
> 1 structural engineer 2 Skyscrapers 3 urban sprawl
> 4 green belt 5 outskirts 6 amenities 7 conservation

2 Learners complete the sentences with their own ideas. Monitor to help with language and refer learners back to the reading texts if they have no ideas or are unsure about vocabulary and spelling. Learners compare answers with a partner. Check answers with the class. Learners record useful words.

> **Possible answers**
>
> 1 … to design environmentally-friendly, cost-effective buildings.
> 2 … to consider their environmental impact.
> 3 … it is important to protect our heritage.
> 4 … it protects the countryside from urban sprawl.
> 5 … sewers, municipal buildings and sports facilities.
> 6 … it increases people's dependence on cars.

CRITICAL THINKING

Give learners a minute to read the Writing task they will do at the end of the unit (a persuasive essay, *Which is more important when building a new home: its location or its size?*) and keep it in mind as they do the next exercises.

EVALUATE

1 Focus learners on the arguments and look at the first one as a class. Ask learners if this is an argument which supports the importance of protecting the environment (a), minimizing costs (b), or if it gives them equal importance (c). (It supports minimizing costs.) Learners complete the exercise. They compare answers with a partner. Check answers with the class.

> **Answers**
>
> the environment is more important: 2, 5
> minimizing cost is more important: 1, 4
> both are equally important: 3, 6

ANALYZE

2 Focus learners on the diagrams and ask one to show where he or she would position the first statement. Ask the others if they agree. Although there is no right or wrong exact answer, the number 1 should be on the lower 'Cost' line. Learners evaluate how persuasive they think the arguments are. They compare ideas with a partner, justifying their answers. Check some ideas with the class, but remember there are no right or wrong answers – it depends on personal opinion.

3 Learners now look at the third line and mark their own position on it. They compare their position with a partner and explain their answer.

WRITING

GRAMMAR FOR WRITING

REGISTER IN ACADEMIC WRITING

1 Paraphrase or ask learners to read the information in the box. To check comprehension, ask for examples of slang expressions (e.g. *gotta, you know*), informal phrasal verbs (e.g. *put up with, set up*) and other personal pronouns (e.g. *we, us*) that learners should not use in academic writing. Note that occasionally a phrasal verb is needed in this type of writing as there is no alternative. Learners read the paragraph and match the more informal words in the text to the academic words/phrases, using dictionaries if necessary. They compare with a partner. Check answers with the class.

Answers

1 c 2 i 3 h 4 f 5 a 6 b 7 e 8 g 9 d

2 👤👥 Learners complete the sentences with their own ideas. Monitor to help with language and refer learners back to the reading texts if they have no ideas or are unsure about vocabulary and spelling. Learners compare answers with a partner. Check answers with the class.

Possible answers

1 …provide the space and facilities that are needed.
2 …how much money an eco-friendly building will save in the long term.
3 …the well-being of the local community.
4 …there is plenty of sun.
5 …the people who use the buildings.
6 …constructing ugly buildings.

ACADEMIC WRITING SKILLS

ORDERING INFORMATION

1 👤👥 Paraphrase or ask learners to read the information in the box. Point out that this type of ordering applies to all types of academic writing. Focus learners on the first sentence in the exercise. Ask learners to read options a and b and decide which would be the best follow-on (Sentence a). Elicit why this one is better (the subject of Sentence a – *this lack of space* – relates directly to the word *crowded* at the end of the first sentence. If necessary do another sentence with the whole class to ensure they understand the task. Learners complete the exercise. They compare with a partner. Check answers with the class.

Answers

1 a 2 b 3 a 4 a 5 a

WRITING TASK

WRITING A FIRST DRAFT

1 👤 Focus learners once more on the writing task title. Check they understand it fully by asking the following questions:

- What kind of academic writing task is it? (An essay.)
- How is an essay different from a report? (It is less specific and no recommendations are needed.)

- Should you talk about the beauty of the building in your essay? (No, just its location and size.)
- Where will you find information and ideas to help you write the essay? (In Reading 1, Reading 2 and the Critical thinking section. You can also use your own ideas.)

If learners need help generating ideas, tell them to work in groups to brainstorm more ideas. You could also write the following prompts on the board to help them:

family size / age and sex of children / lifestyle / number of bedrooms / bathrooms / city / village / near family / school / work / shops

Learners look back over the unit and make notes in the plan provided. Remind them to write their arguments in order of persuasiveness in each paragraph. Give learners the opportunity to ask you questions about vocabulary or use dictionaries. Tell them they will not be allowed to use dictionaries while they are writing.

2 👤 Learners write the first draft of their essay following their plans. Allow about 40 minutes for this. They should write at least 250 words and highlight any language (including spelling) of which they are unsure. Give them a warning five minutes before the end of the set time.

EDIT

3 👤 To encourage learners to take responsibility for their own learning, tell them to check their writing using the task checklist. Stress that this is a very important part of the writing process as it helps learners to learn from their mistakes. Encourage them to look back over their plan and at the unit.

4 👤 Learners make any necessary changes to their essays.

5 👤 Learners check their written language now using the language checklist. They can also check any spelling that they were unsure of by looking back over the unit, using a dictionary, or by asking other learners or you. In addition, remind them to check carefully for any errors that they often make in their writing (e.g. particular spellings, subject-verb agreements, omitting verbs, etc.)

6 👤👥 Learners make any other changes and write up their final essays. If comfortable doing so, they can read each other's writing and suggest improvements before handing the essays in to you for marking.

OBJECTIVES REVIEW

See Introduction, page 9 for ideas about using the Objectives review with your learners.

WORDLIST

See Introduction, page 9 for ideas about how to make the most of the Wordlist with your learners.

REVIEW TEST

See page 113 for the photocopiable Review test for this unit and page 92 for ideas about when and how to administer the Review test.

MODEL ANSWER

See page 131 for the photocopiable Model answer.

RESEARCH PROJECT

Create an online architectural tour of a famous building in your country.

Divide the class into groups ask them to think about an online guide or documentary for tourists to their country. Ask them to take pictures or make videos of an interesting architectural building.

Using presentation software or an online tool, they can create an interactive tour of the building with descriptions and photos of architectural features and historical facts. Alternatively they can use a movie app to make their own documentary.

8 ENERGY

Learning objectives

Focus learners on the Learning objectives box and tell them that this is what they will be working on in this unit. Later they will write an essay: *'The world is unable to meet its energy needs. What three sources of renewable energy will be most effective in solving this problem in your country? Which is your preferred option?'* Show learners this essay title on page 156 but reassure them that all the work in this unit will help them to write it. At the end of the unit they will be able to assess how well they can manage the skills in the Learning objectives box.

UNLOCK YOUR KNOWLEDGE

Lead-in

👥 Learners work in groups. They imagine that they have got lost in the desert. It is mid-afternoon and very hot and sunny, but it will be very cold when the sun goes down so they need to make a fire. They have no matches, lighter or glass with them. However, they do have a can of cola and a bar of chocolate. Around them there are some small pieces of wood. Learners discuss how they can light a fire with only these objects. Allow five minutes for discussion. Learners share their ideas with the rest of the class. If nobody gives the correct answer, explain it using the answer below.

Answer

It is claimed that you can start a fire by rubbing the bottom of a drinks can with chocolate to make it smooth and shiny. You alternate rubbing with chocolate and rubbing with the chocolate wrapper (it does not matter what this is made of). You may have to do this for up to an hour! Once the bottom of the can is very shiny, you point it at the sun with a piece of the chocolate wrapper held to it. The sun will soon reflect strongly enough to set the paper on fire. You use that to light a small piece of wood and then bigger ones. Warning, should your learners ever try to do this, they should not eat the chocolate as it will be full of aluminium!

👥 👥 Learners discuss the questions in pairs or small groups. Monitor to help with vocabulary, encourage participation and check learners' level of existing knowledge on the topic. Check some ideas with the class.

Answers

1, 3 and 4 Answers will vary.
2 *Fossil fuels:* fuels which were formed underground from plant and animal remains millions of years ago.
Renewable energy: energy that is produced using the sun, wind, etc.

WATCH AND LISTEN

Video script

ALTERNATIVE ENERGY

As the world's population increases, so too does the demand for energy. Traditionally energy resources have been non-renewable fossil fuels such as oil, coal and gas. As they begin to run out, the search for cleaner, renewable energy resources becomes more urgent.

Solar energy and biofuels are just two of many alternative energies that could help solve the world's energy crisis. As with traditional fossil fuels, large solar power plants can be built to supply energy directly to a country's national electricity network. But solar power can also work on a much smaller scale. In Mount Pleasant, Washington the whole neighbourhood formed a co-operative, a volunteer community organization, so that everyone could benefit from solar energy. Many of the residents had solar panels installed on their roofs. As a result they benefit from free electricity at source, and they can sell any electricity they don't use back to the power company. This resident has saved 80% on his electricity bill!

Transport and travel are a huge drain on the world's energy resources, so it is important to find an alternative, renewable energy source for cars. Biofuel can be used as a replacement for petrol and diesel and is being produced using canola flowers. These flowers can be grown close to the end user so transport costs are low, and energy wastage limited. They are also carbon neutral: the amount of carbon they produce when burnt is equal to the amount they absorb when growing.

With most countries still very reliant on old forms of energy, both individuals and governments face a huge challenge. But the developments in solar and biofuel energies give us hope for a cleaner future.

PREPARING TO WATCH

UNDERSTANDING KEY VOCABULARY

1 👤👥 Learners match the words to the definitions using a dictionary if necessary. Learners compare answers with a partner. Check answers with the class. Model and drill vocabulary as necessary.

Answers

1 b (Note: *petrol* is called *gas* or *gasoline* in American English.) 2 f (the prefix *hydro-* means water) 3 d 4 a 5 c 6 g 7 e (the prefix *bio-* means connected with life and living things)

2 👤👥 Focus learners on the table and check they remember the difference between fossil fuels and renewable energy. Elicit where *petrol* should be written as an example (*fossil* fuels as it comes from oil). Learners continue the exercise alone. They compare answers with a partner. Check answers with the class.

Answers

fossil fuels: petrol, diesel
renewable energy: hydroelectricity, solar power, canola oil, wind turbine, biofuel

WHILE WATCHING

UNDERSTANDING MAIN IDEAS

3 ▶👤👥 Tell learners they are going to watch a video about alternative energy. Ask if they think it will be about fossil fuels or renewable energy (renewable energy, which is an 'alternative' to more traditional fossil fuels). Learners read the questions and watch the video to check the answers. They compare answers with a partner. Check answers with the class.

Answers

1 Solar power and biofuels.
2 The advantages of the two forms of renewable energy.
3 Both national and local projects.

LISTENING FOR KEY INFORMATION

4 ▶👤👥 Learners try to remember the answers to the questions from the first viewing of the video. They watch again to check their answers and compare with a partner. Check answers with the class.

Answers

1 The population is increasing and we are using more fuel.
2 It formed a solar power co-operative.
3 It can be produced close to the end-user and it is carbon neutral.
4 Finding enough clean fuel to satisfy consumer demand.

5 ▶👥👥👥 Learners read the summary and try to complete it in pairs before watching the video again to check their answers. Weaker groups who do not manage to predict many of the answers may need to have the video paused so they have time to think and write answers. Learners compare with another pair. Check answers with the class.

Answers

1 neighbourhood (In American English there is no *u* – *neighborhood*)
2 benefit
3 sell
4 80
5 cars
6 biofuel
7 canola
8 neutral (Highlight the *neu* spelling if necessary)

WORKING OUT MEANING FROM CONTEXT

6 👥 Learners work with a partner. They discuss what they think the words in bold might mean. Check answers with the class.

Answers

1 The amount of something which is used
2 Different from what has come before
3 A group of people working together towards the same goal
4 An individual's impact on the environment through the production of greenhouse gases
5 No negative impact on the environment through the production of greenhouse gases

DISCUSSION

7 👥👥👥 Learners discuss the questions in pairs or small groups. Give them a few minutes to think about their opinions and language they may need to express them before they start speaking. Monitor to help with vocabulary and to encourage participation. Check a few answers with the class. Encourage learners to respond to each other's ideas.

Answers will vary.

READING 1

PREPARING TO READ

UNDERSTANDING KEY VOCABULARY

1 👤👥 Focus learners on the photograph and ask if they have any know anything about wind turbines or why people might have strong feelings about them (some people feel they spoil the landscape while others find them beautiful). Learners match the energy types with the sources, using a dictionary if necessary. Learners compare answers with a partner. Check answers with the class.

Answers

1 c (remind learners that *hydro-* means water if necessary) 2 d 3 a 4 e (remind learners that *bio-* refers to life or living things) 5 b (*geo-* means relating to the earth and *thermal* means connected to heat)

2 👤👥 Tell learners they are going to read some presentation slides for a lecture. They skim read the texts (allow 2 to 3 minutes for this) and decide which is the best title. Learners compare answers with a partner, saying why they did not choose the other titles. Check answers with the class.

Answers

3 is the best title. 1 is incorrect because the slides are not about fossil fuels, 2 and 4 are incorrect because the slides are about both advantages and disadvantages of fuel types, and 5 is incorrect because the slides are about different forms of renewable energy, not just the concept of conservation.

WHILE READING

READING FOR DETAIL

3 👤👥 Learners read the descriptions and write the type of energy that is being described (some energy types are described twice). They then look back at the presentation slides to check their answers. Learners compare answers in pairs. Check answers with the class.

Answers

1 solar 2 biomass 3 geothermal 4 hydropower
5 solar 6 geothermal 7 wind 8 hydropower

4 👤👥 It is very useful for learners to be able to understand the general themes of an article from a newspaper headline. They read the headlines and match them with one of the energy sources (two types of energy are referred to twice). Learners compare answers with a partner. Check answers with the class.

Answers

1 hydropower 2 wind 3 biomass 4 solar
5 geothermal 6 hydropower 7 biomass

READING BETWEEN THE LINES

WORKING OUT MEANING FROM CONTEXT

5 👤👥 Ask learners what their choices are when they see a word in a reading text that they do not know. (Ignore it and hope it is not too important, guess the meaning from the context, use any pictures to help you to guess, look it up in a dictionary, ask somebody, etc.) Ask learners about the advantages of guessing meaning from context. (A dictionary is not always available, you are more likely to remember the word if you have thought about it, etc.) Ask learners what the disadvantages are (not always possible to guess a word, especially if there are many unknown words in the text, you may be wrong etc.) Paraphrase or ask learners to read the information in the box. Learners read the words in the first column and try to work out which is the closest synonym in meaning. They should not use dictionaries. They compare answers. Check answers with the class.

Answers

1 rubbish: waste (*Leftovers* refer to uneaten food and *ruins* are buildings that are falling down.)
2 aquatic: found in water (*Aqua-* is a prefix meaning *water.*)
3 offshore: in the sea (The *shore* is where the land meets the sea.)
4 inexhaustible: unlimited (*Exhaust* means use all of something so there is none left. *Inexhaustible* means it can never be exhausted.)
5 initial: original (*Initial* refers to the beginning of something. The first letters of your names are your *initials.*)
6 generate: produce (*Generate* is often used with *energy.*)
7 universally: everywhere
8 store: keep (When you *acquire* something you start to own it, when you *supply* something you usually sell it.)

DISCUSSION

6 👥 👥👥 Learners discuss the questions in pairs or small groups. Give them a few minutes to think about their opinions and language they may need to express them before they start speaking. Monitor to help with vocabulary and to encourage participation. Check a few answers with the class. Encourage learners to respond to each other's ideas.

> Answers will vary.

READING 2

PREPARING TO READ

USING YOUR KNOWLEDGE TO PREDICT CONTENT

1 👤👥 Set the scene for the next text by reminding learners that we are using resources faster than we can replace them (*if* they are replaceable). Go through the example of what will happen when we start running out of oil. Ask if learners can think of any more consequences of this. Allow them a few minutes to think about their answers to the other natural resources. They then discuss their suggestions in pairs and write their ideas, as in the example. Monitor to help with language and prompt with ideas if necessary. Check ideas with the class. Encourage learners to respond to each other's ideas.

> **Possible answers**
>
> 2 Droughts, problems with growing crops and the death of livestock and other animals.
> 3 Less food and habitat for animals; flooding due to excess water run-off.
> 4 Food prices would rise and there could be riots, starvation and death.
> 5 Prices of metals would rise sharply; consumer goods would be more expensive.

2 👤👥 Go through the example of possible solutions to an oil shortage. Ask if learners can think of any more solutions to this problem. Allow them a few minutes to think about their answers to the other resources. Then they discuss their solutions in pairs. After they have discussed each one, they should write their ideas, as in the example. Monitor to help with language and prompt with ideas if necessary.

Check ideas with the class. Encourage learners to respond to each other's ideas.

> **Possible answers**
>
> 2 Build water storage facilities (dams, irrigation channels, etc.)
> 3 Protect forests; create national parks; plant new trees; build dams to stop serious flooding.
> 4 Reduce food waste through education; encourage people to eat produce that needs less land, fishing quotas.
> 5 Find new sources of metal; ensure that metal is recycled from old items.

3 👥 Tell learners to look at the essay title. They discuss in pairs what they think it means and think of examples of what can be reduced, reused or recycled.

> Answers will vary.

4 👤👥 Learners read to check their answers. Discourage dictionary use at this stage. Learners check in pairs. Check answers with the class.

> **Possible answers**
>
> *Reduce* means to consume and use less. We can reduce our use of electricity, petrol and chemicals for example.
> *Re-use* means to use things again, for example, plastic bags from the supermarket, or plastic containers.
> *Recycle* means to collect and treat rubbish in order to produce useful materials. Paper, glass, and some metals and plastics can be recycled.

> **Optional activity**
>
> Point out that all three verbs start with the prefix *re-*. Ask learners what this often means (*again*). Ask learners for some more words that begin with the prefix *re-*: *rewrite, repaint, reconsider, redevelop, refill, refresh* etc. Point out that re-use has a hyphen (-) whereas the other words do not. Ask why (*use* starts with a vowel). Learners record any useful words.

WHILE READING

READING FOR DETAIL

5 👤 Learners match the words from the two columns to make collocations. They do as many as they can without looking back at the essay and then check in the text to see if they were right. With a weak group do feedback at this stage, but with a stronger one, let them go directly to the next exercise.

> **Answers**
>
> 1 e 2 f 3 a 4 c 5 g 6 b 7 d

6 Learners read the sentences and complete them with the collocations in Exercise 5. Learners compare answers with a partner. Check answers with the class.

Answers

1 adopt a strategy 2 motorized transport 3 wasteful practices 4 address the problem 5 urgent action 6 alarming rate 7 electrical items

READING BETWEEN THE LINES

MAKING INFERENCES FROM THE TEXT

7 Learners read the questions and come to their own conclusions before discussing with a partner. Check ideas with the class.

Possible answers

1 They are unlikely to change their habits unless it affects them financially.
2 It produces a lot of carbon emissions.
3 It does not require as much additional energy as changing the state of the resources.
4 The occurrence of natural disasters like flooding are increasing in many parts of the world.

DISCUSSION

8 Learners discuss the questions in pairs or small groups. Give them a few minutes to think about their opinions and language they may need to express them before they start speaking. Check that they understand the words *penalize* (punish) and this meaning of *generation* (all the people of about the same age within a society). Monitor to help with vocabulary and to encourage participation. Check a few answers with the class. Encourage learners to respond to each other's ideas.

Answers will vary.

⊙ LANGUAGE DEVELOPMENT

ENERGY COLLOCATIONS

1 Remind learners that collocations are content words usually used together, so it is helpful to learn some to make their writing and speaking sound more natural. Focus learners on set number one. Ask learners which word

from the above could follow all of these words to make collocations. They could try saying the possible collocations out loud – some may sound right or sound wrong to them. Establish that the first answer is *fuel*. Learners complete the activity They compare answers with a partner. Check answers with the class. Learners record useful words.

Answers

1 fuel 2 energy 3 pollution 4 source 5 production 6 problem

Optional activity

Learners look through all the words in Exercise 1 and highlight all the ones that end with the sound /əl/. They then write the words in four columns according to how the /əl/ sound is spelled (see below for endings). Ask what the parts of speech of these words are. Can they see any patterns? Learners compare answers with a partner. Check answers with the class.

Answers

-al	-le	-el	-il
geothermal environmental industrial agricultural medical	renewable	diesel fuel	fossil
Adjectives, especially longer, more academic ones are likely to end in -al.	Adjectives also often end with -able or -ible. Other words ending with -le can also be nouns (most common), verbs (especially when they are the same as the noun) and some other adjectives.	Over 80% of words ending in -el are nouns.	Words ending in -il for the sound /əl/ are much less common, but are usually nouns.

Learners look at either Reading 2 on page 148 or some academic writing from their own field of study and find more examples of words ending with the /əl/ sound. They check which of the spelling patterns the words follow.

2 Learners complete the sentences with words from the previous exercise. Encourage them to check the spelling carefully. They compare answers with a partner. Check answers with the class.

Answers

1 nuclear 2 health/medical 3 source 4 Fossil 5 Alternative 6 water 7 solar 8 radioactive

FORMAL AND INFORMAL ACADEMIC VERBS

3 👥 👥👥 Ask learners what kind of verbs they should avoid using in their academic writing (informal ones, such as phrasal verbs, where possible). Learners match the formal verbs with the informal ones, using a dictionary if necessary. They check with a partner. Check answers with the class.

> ### Answers
> 1 d 2 h 3 g 4 f 5 c 6 b 7 a 8 e

4 👥👥 Learners complete the sentences with the formal verbs from Exercise 3. Before they do this check understanding of the following: a *debate* (a serious discussion of a subject in which many people take part) and *advocate* (someone who publicly and strongly supports something). Learners check answers in pairs. Check answers with the class. Learners record useful words.

> ### Answers
> 1 diminish 2 deliver 3 contested 4 consult 5 instigate
> 6 utilizes 7 omit 8 secure

CRITICAL THINKING

Give learners a minute to read the Writing task they will do at the end of the unit (a problem-solving essay, *The world is unable to meet its energy needs. What three sources of renewable energy will be most effective in solving this problem in your country? Which is your preferred option?*) and keep it in mind as they do the next exercises.

EVALUATE

1 👤👥 Focus learners on the questionnaire, which they answer by writing *yes* or *no* depending on their beliefs. They also have to give a reason for their answer and say how it relates to their own country. They can refer back to the reading texts if they need to but need to paraphrase, rather than copy from them. If you think your learners will find this exercise difficult, they could do it in pairs.

2 👥👥 Learners discuss their questionnaire with a partner (or with another pair if they have already worked with a partner) and discuss their differences. Tell them that they can 'borrow' each other's ideas for the essay.

UNDERSTAND

3 👤👥 Paraphrase or ask learners to read the information in the box. Learners use the ideas that they had in Exercise 1 to rank the energy sources according to suitability for their country. They should be prepared to justify their answers. They compare answers.

4 👤👥 In the essay learners will need to write about three sources of energy so they focus on these here. Refer them to the example or the Reading text for help but stress that they should use their own words. Learners show their ideas to a partner and help each other with any language problems. Check some ideas with the class, but stress there are no right or wrong answers.

WRITING

GRAMMAR FOR WRITING

RELATIVE CLAUSES

1 👤👥 Paraphrase or ask learners to read the information in the box. To check comprehension, display the sentence and ask the questions.

- *This is the energy source which would be most suitable for my country.* Where is the relative clause in this sentence?
- Why do we use a relative clause in this sentence? (to define the energy source that we are writing about)
- What is the relative pronoun in the sentence? (*which*)
- Which relative pronouns could you use after the following subjects? *Dubai* (*where* or *which*), *Friday* (*when* or *which*), *Mohammed* (*who* or *whose*), *happiness* (*which*).

Learners complete the sentences with one of the relative pronouns from the box and highlight the whole relative clause. They compare answers in pairs. Check answers with the class.

> ### Answers
> 1 who 2 whose 3 where 4 when 5 which

2 👤👥 Focus learners on the sentences in Exercise 1. Ask how Sentences 1 and 5 differ from the others (the relative clause is between commas). Focus on Sentence 2. Ask learners which people worry about radioactive leaks (only those who live near nuclear power stations). Then ask what the difference would be if we put commas after *people* and after *stations* (it would refer to people we have already mentioned, the fact that they live near nuclear power stations would then just be extra information). This information between commas is part of a non-defining relative clause. Paraphrase or ask learners to read the information in the next box. Note that in some grammar resources these are called *identifying* and *non-identifying* relative clauses.

Learners continue the exercise. They compare answers with a partner. Check answers with the class.

Answers

1 no commas required
2 Solar power, which is a form of renewable energy, is very popular in southern Spain.
3 no commas required
4 no commas required
5 no commas required
6 Al Gore, who is a key supporter of alternative energy, won the Nobel prize in 2007.

PHRASES TO INTRODUCE ADVANTAGES AND DISADVANTAGES

3 👤👥 Paraphrase or ask learners to read the information in the box. Learners note which adjectives make the assertion stronger and which make it weaker. (Stronger: *huge, most obvious, most serious, distinct, inherent.* Weaker: *apparent, possible, potential.*) Learners write the sentences, making them stronger or weaker. They compare with a partner. Check answers with the class.

Possible answers

1 The most serious disadvantage of biomass is that it produces greenhouse gases.
2 Another potential disadvantage of biomass is that large areas of land are needed.
3 The most obvious advantage of hydropower is that energy can be stored and used when it is needed.
4 An apparent disadvantage of geothermal energy is that it is only available in certain places.
5 One huge advantage of wind power is that it creates zero pollution.
6 A further possible advantage of wind power is that it is relatively cheap.

ACADEMIC WRITING SKILLS

EDITING LANGUAGE

1 👤 Ask learners why they need to edit their work. When they have finished a piece of work they need to 'tidy up' their writing by editing it for language errors.) Point out that while they are studying English, editing will help them to learn if they keep a list of their errors so they do not repeat them.

Paraphrase or ask learners to read the information in the box. Learners try to write the correct prepositions in the text. Learners compare with a partner. Check answers with the class.

Answers

1 of 2 with 3 at 4 in/at 5 on 6 with/by 7 towards/into 8 from/in 9 since 10 about

2 👤👥 Paraphrase or ask learners to read the information in the box. Before doing this task, learners look back at previous writing they have done and identify some of their typical spelling error in pairs or small groups if appropriate. Monitor to see which spelling error types they have found and why they suggest they made them.

Focus learners on the first sentence of the exercise. Ask them to find the spelling mistakes in the sentences. Point out that these may involve a wrong letter, a missing or added letter, or letters in the wrong order. Learners find the errors in the first sentence (*unclear, broblem, enviroment*). Learners continue the exercise in pairs. Check answers with the class.

Answers

1 **Nuclear** power poses a serious **problem** for the **environment.**
2 It is **unclear which type** of alternative energy is best.
3 **Too many people nowadays** are not responsible enough in their energy usage.
4 Not **enough** people **know** how they can improve **their** behaviour.
5 **By** leading **comfortable** lives, people may be endangering **future** generations.
6 **Alternative** energy is much friendlier to the environment **than** fossil fuels **because** it is renewable.
7 It is **believed** that the place **where** solar energy **would** be most effective is the Sahara.
8 **Governments** won't change their policies **until** there is demand **from** people.

COUNTABLE AND UNCOUNTABLE NOUNS

3 👤👥👥 Check learners are clear that countable nouns refer to things that can be used with a number. Uncountable nouns cannot be used with numbers. Learners match the countable and uncountable nouns in the exercise. They compare with a partner. Check answers with the class.

> **Answers**
>
> 1 c 2 e 3 f 4 b 5 d 6 a 7 g 8 h

4 👤👥👥 Learners do the exercise. Point out that they can make the countable nouns plural when necessary. Learners compare with a partner and justify their answers. Check answers with the class.

> **Answers**
>
> 1 luggage 2 feedback/comments 3 programs
> 4 academic papers 5 things 6 furniture 7 tools/
> equipment 8 flat

WRITING TASK

WRITING A FIRST DRAFT

1 👤 Focus learners once more on the writing task title. Check they understand it fully by asking the following questions:

- Should you discuss whether the first sentence is true in your essay? (No, you have to accept the first sentence is true.)
- Should you discuss the use of fossil fuels in your country? (No. The main body of the essay is about renewable energy.)
- What do you need to consider about your own country? (The weather, geography, population, etc.)
- Should you give your opinion? (Yes, you give your opinion about your preferred options.)
- Where will you find information and ideas to help you? (In the unit, but Reading 1 and the Critical thinking section will be particularly useful)

Learners look at the structure given and then look back over the unit and choose three types of energy that are suitable for their country. They make notes, using the structure provided. Give learners the opportunity to ask you questions about vocabulary or use dictionaries. Tell them

they will not be allowed to use dictionaries while they are writing.

2 👤 Learners write the essay. Allow about 40 minutes for this. They should write at least 250 words. They should highlight any language (including spelling) of which they are unsure. Give them a warning five minutes before the end of the set time.

EDIT

3–6 👤 To encourage learners to take responsibility for their own learning, tell them to check their writing using the task checklist. Stress that this is a very important part of the writing process as it helps learners to learn from their mistakes. Encourage them to look back over their plan and at the unit.

OBJECTIVES REVIEW

See Introduction, page 9 for ideas about using the Objectives review with your learners.

WORDLIST

See Introduction, page 9 for ideas about how to make the most of the Wordlist with your learners.

REVIEW TEST

See page 116 for the photocopiable Review test for this unit and page 92 for ideas about when and how to administer the Review test.

MODEL ANSWER

See page 132 for the photocopiable Model answer.

RESEARCH PROJECT

Transform an area of your learning environment so that it is more energy efficient.

Ask the class to find ways to reduce their energy usage in their learning environment. They may want to look at areas such as air conditioning / heating alternatives, lighting, insulation, energy efficiency guides, electrical equipment etc.

Tell learners that they have to start a campaign to change an area of their learning environment and encourage others to do the same. They need to think of marketing, branding, issuing information and presentations etc.

9 ART AND DESIGN

Learning objectives

Focus learners on the Learning objectives box and tell them that this is what they will be working on in this unit. Later they will write an essay titled: *'Fashion, cooking, video games and sport have all been likened to fine art. Choose one of these and discuss whether it should be considered fine art, comparable to painting or literature.'* Show learners this essay title on page 173 but reassure them that all the work in this unit will help them to write it. At the end of the unit they will be able to assess how well they can manage the skills in the Learning objectives box.

UNLOCK YOUR KNOWLEDGE

Lead-in

👥 Learners choose an object from the classroom or from their personal possessions that they have with them. They show their group and discuss which features of it are purely functional (they exist because they do a job), which are non-functional (only included for decorative purposes), and which are a combination. For example, on a pair of trainers a blue stripe may only be decorative whereas a yellow one may help the wearer be seen better. The treads on the bottom of the shoe are functional, but the design of the treads may be decorative.

👥👥 Learners discuss the questions in pairs or small groups. Monitor to help with vocabulary, encourage participation and check learners' level of existing knowledge on the topic. Check some ideas with the class.

> Answers will vary.

WATCH AND LISTEN

Video script

ART AND DESIGN

Narrator: Leonardo da Vinci was a genius. He is famous today as a great painter but he was also a sculptor, architect, musician, mathematician, engineer, writer, scientist and inventor. His inventions were hundreds of years ahead of their time but many were never made.

This team of engineers is going to put a Leonardo da Vinci design to the test using the materials which were available 500 years ago.

The engineers are shown da Vinci's design of a self-propelled cart. They immediately see a problem. da Vinci didn't complete the design and it's unclear whether the cart should have three or five wheels. The team decides to split into two to test both designs. They suggest a race to find the winner.

First they use a computer to turn their interpretation of da Vinci's design into modern engineering plans and then start to make the wheels for the cart. Making the wheels is more difficult than the teams thought. Making the drive mechanism looks even more difficult but while Team 1 cuts the wood with a time-consuming traditional method, Team 2 has a short-cut in mind. They use the laser cutter to save time making the cogs in the mechanism. Da Vinci's design used metal springs to provide power for the mechanism but Team 1 is nervous when they wind their powerful spring as it could break the cart or cause an injury.

The other team manages to get both springs working and their cart is finished.

On the evening of the race both teams wind the springs in their carts. However Team 2 loses count and winds the spring up too much, breaking it. They decide to run the race on one spring anyway.

The result is in no doubt. While Team 2's cart starts quicker, their lack of power means that Team 1 wins the race comfortably. The teams prove the genius of Leonardo da Vinci's 500 year old design.

PREPARING TO WATCH

USING VISUALS TO PREDICT CONTENT

1 👥 Focus learners on the pictures from the video. Learners discuss the questions in small groups. Check ideas with the class, but do not give any answers at this stage as the questions will be answered in the video.

UNDERSTANDING KEY VOCABULARY

2 👤👥 Learners match the words to the definitions, using a dictionary if necessary. Learners compare answers with a partner. Check answers with the class.

> **Answers**
> 1 j 2 e 3 d 4 b 5 h 6 c 7 i 8 a 9 g 10 f

3 ▶ 👤👥 Tell learners they are going to watch a video about one of Leonardo da Vinci's designs. Learners watch the video and check their answers to the questions in Exercise 1. They compare answers with a partner. Check answers with the class.

Answers

1 He was an Italian Renaissance artist and inventor who lived about 500 years ago. His most famous painting is the Mona Lisa.
2 People are amazed that he had modern ideas hundreds of years ago and they want to see if they will work.
3 A self-propelled cart or an early kind of wind-up car.
4 They are using traditional materials, but one team uses modern equipment.
5 They are going to test out the cart.

WHILE WATCHING

UNDERSTANDING MAIN IDEAS

4 ▶ 👤👥 Tell learners they are going to watch the video again. First, they look at the events and try to remember the order of them. Learners watch the video to check their answers. They compare with a partner. Check answers with the class.

Answers
1 d 2 c 3 h 4 b 5 f 6 e 7 g 8 a

LISTENING FOR KEY INFORMATION

5 ▶ 👤👥 Learners say whether the statements are true or false before watching again. They watch the video to check. In Question 4 point out that *have little difficulty* means that they find it quite easy (whereas *have a little difficulty* would mean that they did not find it easy). Learners compare with a partner, saying what is wrong with the false statements. Check answers with the class.

Answers
1 T 2 F (His designs were innovative and ahead of their time.) 3 F (The design is difficult to follow.) 4 F (Making the wheels is more difficult than the teams thought.) 5 F (Only one team uses a laser cutter.) 6 F (They only break one of the springs.) 7 F (They broke it because they made a mistake when counting the number of turns.)

RESPONDING TO THE VIDEO CONTENT

6 👥 Learners discuss the questions with a partner. Check ideas with the class.

Possible answers

1 The race is not fair because one cart operated on half power.
2 They used computer-aided design, modern steel tools and a laser cutter.
3 He may have intended it for military use. It was an innovative idea for the time, one of the first prototypes of a car.

DISCUSSION

7 👥 👥 Learners discuss the questions in pairs or small groups. Give them a few minutes to think about their opinions and language they may need to express them before they start speaking. Monitor to help with vocabulary and to encourage participation. Check a few answers with the class. Encourage learners to respond to each other's ideas.

Answers will vary.

Possible answers

1 They learned how difficult it is to recreate a machine from a 500-year-old design and that da Vinci's design actually worked.
2 da Vinci did not have scientific knowledge of flight and wooden machines would not have worked.
3 We know so much about each academic subject now that it is no longer possible to be an expert in more than a few areas.

READING 1

PREPARING TO READ

UNDERSTANDING KEY VOCABULARY

1 👤👥 Learners match the materials and objects with the art forms, using dictionaries to complete the activity if necessary. Learners compare with a partner. Check answers with the class.

Answers
1 music 2 furniture making 3 pottery 4 calligraphy 5 sculpture 6 poetry 7 photography 8 weaving

USING YOUR KNOWLEDGE TO PREDICT CONTENT

2 👤👥 Learners read the descriptions and match the pictures to the artist. They compare answers with a partner. Check answers with the class.

Answers

1 b 2 d 3 a 4 c

3 👤👥 Paraphrase or ask learners to read the information in the box. Ask them what kind of text they would normally scan (any where they are looking for a specific piece of information). Learners scan the magazine article and put the artists in the order they appear in it. They compare answers with a partner, remembering to talk about the pictures too. Check answers with the class.

Answers

1 a Andy Warhol
2 d Frank Lloyd Wright
3 c Marcel Duchamp
4 b Damien Hirst

READING FOR DETAIL

4 👤👥 Learners read the statements and decide if they are *true*, *false* or it *does not say*. Learners compare answers with a partner, saying what is wrong with the false statements. Check answers with the class.

Answers

1 T 2 F (It is an example of applied art.) 3 T 4 DNS (We do not know if he was the first person to say it.) 5 DNS (It says he was famous for Pop Art, it does not say if he invented it.) 6 F (Frank Lloyd Wright was talking about fine art.) 7 DNS 8 F (He gets his assistants to make it, although he has the ideas himself.)

READING BETWEEN THE LINES

5 👤👥 Focus learners on the first statement and ask them which artist they think would probably say it. The paraphrased answers are in the text (Damian Hirst). Learners complete the exercise. They compare answers with a partner. Check answers with the class.

Answers

1 DH 2 AW 3 MD 4 DH 5 FLW

DISCUSSION

6 👥👥👥 Learners discuss the questions. Monitor to help with vocabulary and to encourage participation. Check a few answers with the class. Encourage learners to respond to each other's ideas.

Answers will vary.

READING 2

PREPARING TO READ

USING YOUR KNOWLEDGE TO PREDICT CONTENT

1 👤👥 Learners read the words in the box and decide which activities they think are art. Stress that there are no right or wrong answers here. Learners discuss with a partner. Check answers with the class. Remind learners that this will be the topic of their writing task later.

UNDERSTANDING KEY VOCABULARY

2 👤👥 Learners match the words with their definitions using a dictionary if necessary. Learners compare answers with a partner. Check answers with the class. Model and drill any words that you think learners will find useful.

Answers

1 c 2 a 3 e 4 i 5 b 6 h 7 d 8 f 9 g

WHILE READING

SCANNING TO FIND INFORMATION

3 👤👥 Focus learners on the essay title and recap on what their answers were in Exercise 1. Learners scan the essay to find which paragraph discusses each of the points. Discourage dictionary use at this stage. Learners compare with a partner. Check answers with the class.

Answers

1 A 2 D 3 B 4 C 5 A 6 B

PARAPHRASING

4 👤👥 Remind learners that paraphrasing is saying the same thing in a different way. They match the sentences from the text and the paraphrases. Learners compare answers with a partner. Check answers with the class.

Answers

1 d 2 c 3 a 4 e 5 b

READING BETWEEN THE LINES

MAKING INFERENCES FROM THE TEXT

5 👤👥 Learners read the statements and decide which person would agree with each opinion. They will need to refer back to the text to do this. Learners compare answers with a partner. Check answers with the class.

> **Answers**
>
> 1 c 2 f 3 a 4 e 5 d 6 b

DISCUSSION

6 👥👥👥 Learners discuss the questions. Monitor to help with vocabulary and to encourage participation. Check a few answers with the class. Encourage learners to respond to each other's ideas.

> **Answers will vary.**

👁 LANGUAGE DEVELOPMENT

QUOTATIONS AND REPORTING INFORMATION

1 👤👥 Paraphrase or ask learners to read the information in the box. To introduce the idea of using quotations, ask learners some of these questions:

- Why should you use quotes in your academic writing? (It can support your arguments, give examples and show that you have read about the subject.)
- What is the difference between *quoting* and *paraphrasing*? (When you quote you write the other person's exact words and use quotation marks. When you paraphrase you write what that person said in your own words and no quotation marks are needed.)
- Do you need to say who originally said something if you quote or paraphrase? (Yes, definitely, for both. If not you may be accused of plagiarism – cheating by pretending that you said something that somebody else said – a very serious matter that can result in failing an assignment or even being expelled from a course.)

- How do you choose quotations? (Use ones that support what you want to say. Make sure you comment on the quotation in your writing.)

Learners use the verbs in the box to complete paraphrases of quotations. They read Quotation 1 and decide whether the Head Teacher felt strongly or not (strongly because the words *absolutely essential* are used). They decide which verb to use in the paraphrase below and put it into the correct form (*insisted* or *argued*). Learners complete the exercise. They check with a partner. Check answers with the class. Learners record useful words.

> **Answers**
>
> 1 insist/argue 2 suggested 3 argued 4 denied
> (note that *denied* means said that you had not done something so it is used with a positive verb)

2 👤👥 Point out that quotations are often not used in full. Learners look at the example quotation and note how the writer has used them in the sentence below. They create sentences using some or all of the words in each quotation. Monitor to check that learners have used appropriate verbs and punctuation. Learners compare answers with a partner. Check some answers with the class.

> **Suggested answers**
>
> 1 Horace said a picture is like a 'poem without words'.
> 2 Bradbury suggested that thought was 'the enemy of creativity'.
> 3 Henri Matisse argued that 'creativity takes courage'.

3 👥 In this exercise learners paraphrase what somebody else has said, using key words but trying to find synonyms where possible. Learners work in pairs to decide what each quotation means and rephrase it in their own words. Monitor closely to help with language and content. Learners compare answers with another pair. Check answers with the class.

> **Suggested answers**
>
> 1 Edward be Bono explained that to become creative we need to change our habits and the way we see the world around us.
> 2 Dee Hock implies that you cannot be creative if you are thinking or worrying about too many things.
> 3 Scott Adams suggested that those who feel they must do everything perfectly cannot be creative.

DESCRIBING ART

Lead-in

Focus learners on the art images on page 162. Ask them to decide on three adjectives to describe each piece of art or their reaction to it. They share their ideas with the class. Encourage learners to respond to each other's ideas.

4 Learners match the adjectives to the definitions, using a dictionary if necessary. They check with a partner. Check answers with the class. Learners record useful words.

Answers

1 c 2 e 3 d 4 b 5 a 6 g 7 h 8 f

5 Learners complete the sentences with words from Exercise 3. They compare answers with a partner. Check answers with the class.

Answers

1 monumental 2 moving 3 decorative 4 lifelike
5 avant-garde 6 Abstract 7 figurative 8 expressive

Optional activity

Focus learners on the adjectives *decorative*, *figurative* and *expressive*. Ask the following questions:

- What do these adjectives have in common in terms of spelling and pronunciation? (They all end in *-ive* and are pronounced /ɪv/. Check that learners are pronouncing this ending with a short *i* sound.)
- Do you know any other adjectives ending in *-ive*? (*descriptive, native, comparative, active, administrative, attractive, creative, effective, expensive* and many more)

Suggest learners keep a list of these adjectives and add to it when they find more.

CRITICAL THINKING

Give learners a minute to read the Writing task they will do at the end of the unit (an essay using supporting quotations, *Fashion, cooking, video games and sport have all been likened to fine art. Choose one of these and discuss whether it should be considered fine art, comparable to painting or sculpture.*) and keep it in mind as they do the next exercises.

UNDERSTAND

1 Learners read the first quotation and decide whether this supports or challenges (disagrees with) the idea that these activities could be considered art. (It challenges it.). They continue the activity, ticking the appropriate column. Learners compare answers with a partner. Check answers with the class.

Answers

1 challenge 2 support 3 challenge 4 support
5 support 6 challenge 7 challenge 8 support

EVALUATE

2 Give learners a few minutes to think about whether they agree with the quotations or not, and why. Then they discuss their reactions with their partner, justifying their ideas. Monitor to help with language, dealing with spelling too as they may need to write these words in their essays. There is no need to get feedback on this at this stage.

3 Focus learners on the example sentence. They delete either *agree* or *disagree* to reflect their opinion and write the reason for this. Learners complete the exercise. Note: in their essays learners should avoid using personal pronouns such as *I*. Learners compare answers with a partner. Check some ideas as a class. Encourage learners to respond to each other's ideas.

WRITING

GRAMMAR FOR WRITING

SUBSTITUTION

1 Paraphrase or ask learners to read the information in the box. Explain or elicit that *substitution* means changing one thing for another. Learners read the paragraph and identify any pronouns or phrases that are used to replace the full name of the car. Do the first example together (*the two-seater roadster*). Learners complete the task. They compare answers with a partner. Check answers with the class.

Answers

The Jaguar E-type is probably one of the most famous cars ever produced. The two-seater roadster was the fastest production sports car on the market in 1961. It was designed to be an expressive mixture of a racing car and something you could use every day. The aerodynamic styling of the car is functional yet beautiful. The bullet shape of the E-type contrasts with the body's curves. The machine's most prominent feature is the long, projecting bonnet which contains the powerful engine. The view of the car's shape is as beautiful from the driving seat as it is to the pedestrian. It is easy to see why Enzo Ferrari called it 'the most beautiful car in the world'.

ELLIPSIS

2 👤👥 Paraphrase or ask learners to read the information in the box. Explain that ellipsis means leaving words out of a sentence without removing any key information from it. Focus learners on the picture. Ask if they recognize or know anything about it. If not you could ask when they think it was painted and why the artist painted it. Tell them they will find out when they read the text. Check that learners know that *Sotheby's* is an art auction house. Learners read the text, crossing out any repetition or words that are not needed and adding in any substitutions where necessary. It is important that there is no loss of information and that the sentences remain grammatically correct. Learners check with a partner. Check answers with the class.

Answers

The Scream is the popular name given to each of four paintings ~~of the Scream~~ by the artist Edvard Munch who painted ~~the scream~~ *them* between 1893 and 1910. The pictures ~~of the scream~~ show a figure against a landscape with a red sky. The National Gallery, Oslo, holds one painting ~~of the Scream~~, the Munch Museum holds two more ~~paintings of the scream~~ and the fourth version ~~of the Scream~~ sold for $119m at Sotheby's on 2 May 2012. To explain the picture ~~of the Scream~~ the artist ~~Edvard Munch~~ wrote in his diary: 'One evening I felt tired and ill. I stopped and looked out over the sea—the sun was setting, and the clouds were turning blood red. I sensed a scream passing through nature; it seemed to me that I heard ~~the scream~~ *it*.'

ACADEMIC WRITING SKILLS

COHERENCE

1 👤👥 Tell learners that if something is coherent it means the parts of it fit together in a natural or sensible way. Paraphrase or ask learners to read the information in the box, focusing on the four different types of words that can make writing coherent. Learners complete the paragraph. They compare answers with a partner. Check answers with the class.

Answers

1 Although 2 because 3 they 4 them 5 They 6 in the same way 7 objects

2 👤👥👥 Learners read the sentences about classic cars (old cars which are still popular although they are no longer produced). They rewrite the sentences as a coherent paragraph, using the devices in the previous exercise writing the sentences in the same order and including all the information. Encourage them to rewrite the paragraph rather than just inserting the words, to check they make appropriate changes to punctuation.

Possible answer

In some cases, there are similarities between cars and fine art, **because** some classic cars are as rare and as expensive as fine art. **For example**, a 1962 Ferrari GTO (a classic car) made $35 million in a sale in 2012. **Although** classic cars are not always a practical means of transport, according to some, classic cars have a personality. **They** describe their feelings towards their classic car as 'love'.

WRITING TASK

WRITING A FIRST DRAFT

1 👤 Focus learners once more on the writing task title. Check they understand it fully by asking the following questions:

- What kind of academic writing task is it? (An essay.)
- Can you give your own opinions? (Yes.)

- How many paragraphs should you write? (Four.)
- What is the minimum number of quotations you should use? (Three.)
- Where can you find quotations for the essay? (In this unit, particularly in the Critical thinking section.)

  Learners look back over the unit and make notes, using the structure provided. Give learners the opportunity to ask you questions about vocabulary or use dictionaries. Tell them they will not be allowed to use dictionaries while they are writing.

2 👤 Learners write the first draft of their essay following their plans. Allow about 40 minutes for this. They should write at least 250 words and highlight any language (including spelling) of which they are unsure. Give them a warning five minutes before the end of the set time.

EDIT

3 👤 To encourage learners to take responsibility for their own learning, tell them to check their writing using the task checklist. Stress that this is a very important part of the writing process as it helps learners to learn from their mistakes. Encourage them to look back over their plan and at the unit.

4 👤 Learners make any necessary changes to their essays.

5 👤 Learners check their written language using the language checklist. They can also check any spelling that they were unsure of by looking back over the unit, using a dictionary, or by asking other learners or you. In addition, remind them to check carefully for any errors that they often make in their writing (e.g. particular spellings, subject-verb agreements, omitting verbs, etc.)

6 👤👥 Learners make any other changes and write up their final essays. If comfortable doing so, they can read each other's writing and suggest improvements before handing the essays in to you for marking.

OBJECTIVES REVIEW

See Introduction, page 9 for ideas about using the Objectives review with your learners.

WORDLIST

See Introduction, page 9 for ideas about how to make the most of the Wordlist with your learners.

REVIEW TEST

See page 119 for the photocopiable Review test for this unit and page 92 for ideas about when and how to administer the Review test.

MODEL ANSWER

See page 133 for the photocopiable Model answer.

RESEARCH PROJECT

Plan an arts and crafts exhibition.

Explain to the class that they are going to plan an art exhibition of local artists and crafts. Crafts could include weaving, jewelry making, costumes, leatherwork, metalwork, pottery, etc. Tell them to research local artists and craftspeople, by visiting galleries and searching online. They should look at the artists and their work or the history of the craft. Learners could also interview local artists or craftspeople.

Ask learners to present this information and images of the artists' work or examples of local crafts as part of an exhibition.

10 AGEING

UNLOCK YOUR KNOWLEDGE

Lead-in

👥 Learners think about the oldest person in their extended family, perhaps a grandparent or great aunt or uncle. They describe this person in small groups, mentioning their relationship to the person, their age, character, their role in their family etc. They also discuss how the world has changed in that person's lifetime. Ask some learners to share their story with the class.

👥👥 Learners discuss the questions in pairs or small groups. Monitor to help with language and to encourage participation. Check some answers with the class. Encourage learners to respond to each other's ideas.

> Answers will vary.

WATCH AND LISTEN

Video script

THE KHANTY OF SIBERIA

The Russian Federation is by far the biggest country in the world. It is twice the size of the United States of America and contains 11 time zones. Siberia is a vast region in the centre and east of the Russian Federation. It is famous for its freezing winters. Temperatures can drop as low as -60C. In the Ugra, in the centre of west Siberia, where temperatures are below freezing for up to seven months of the year, live the Khanty people. The Khanty live as their ancestors lived. A way of life that hasn't changed for centuries.

There are 28,000 Khanty people living today. Alexie and Dulcia Moldanov are among them. They have 200 reindeer. In the coldest months of the year, they keep them in the forest. In the summer the reindeer and the Moldanovs wander together. The Moldanovs live here in the winter, without gas, electricity, or telephones, but they enjoy being outside with their reindeer. But they are getting older and they need help.

Their son Misha lives with his family, in a small village, two hundred miles away. The village has only one road and one shop. Misha and his son Daniil are going to visit Misha's parents. The trip gives Misha the opportunity to teach his six-year-old son about Alexei and Dulcia's traditional way of life. It is a long journey from the village to the forest. Misha and Daniil travel by snowmobile across the snow and ice of Siberia.

There is work for Misha to do. He must repair the reindeer pen in order to stop the animals from escaping. He also helps with rounding the animals up, which is something that Alexie cannot do alone. When Daniil has grown up, Misha will go to live in the forest. Will Daniil one day choose the same life? The future is uncertain. The Khanty way of life is threatened by the modern world. But the more Daniil sees of the forest, the more he will be inspired to protect it.

PREPARING TO WATCH

UNDERSTANDING KEY VOCABULARY

1 👤👥 Learners match words from the box with the definitions, using a dictionary if necessary. Learners compare answers with a partner. Check answers with the class. Model and drill vocabulary as necessary.

> #### Answers
> 1 round up 2 ancestor 3 reindeer, Note the plural is the same as the singular. If culturally appropriate and useful, tell learners reindeer are the animals that pull Santa's sleigh. 4 wander 5 threaten 6 pen 7 inspire

2 👤👥 Learners complete the sentences with words from the previous exercise. They may have to change the form of the words, for example, a verb ending to match the context. They compare answers with a partner. Check answers with the class.

> #### Answers
> 1 Reindeer 2 ancestors 3 threatens 4 pen 5 round up 6 wandered 7 inspired

USING YOUR KNOWLEDGE TO PREDICT CONTENT

3 👥 Tell learners they are going to watch a video about a *tribe* (a group of people, often of related families, who live together, sharing the same language, culture and history). Learners look at the photos and the previous exercises and discuss in pairs whether they think the statements are true or false. Check learners' ideas with the class, but do not give any answers yet. Tell them they will hear the answers when they watch the video.

4 ▶ 👥 Learners watch the video and then discuss with their partner which of their predictions were correct.

> **Answers**
>
> 1 F (They live in Siberia, where the weather is freezing in winter.) 2 F (They live in the countryside.) 3 T 4 T 5 F (It is about three generations of a family.) 6 T

WHILE WATCHING

UNDERSTANDING MAIN IDEAS

5 ▶ 👤👥 Learners read the ideas and watch the video again to put them in the correct order. Learners check their answers in pairs. Check answers with the class.

> **Answers**
>
> 1 b 2 a 3 f 4 g 5 c 6 d 7 e

LISTENING FOR DETAIL

6 ▶ 👤👥 Learners read the sentences and the numbers and try to complete the exercise. Note that 200 is used twice but some numbers are not used at all. Play the first half of the video again for learners to check. Learners compare answers. Check answers with the class.

> **Answers**
>
> 1 11 2 7 3 28,000 4 200 5 200

DISCUSSION

7 👥 👥👥 Learners discuss the questions in pairs or small groups. Give them a few minutes to think about their opinions and language they may need to express them before they start speaking. Monitor to help with vocabulary

and to encourage participation. Check a few answers with the class. Encourage learners to respond to each other's ideas.

> **Answers will vary.**

READING 1

PREPARING TO READ

USING YOUR KNOWLEDGE TO PREDICT CONTENT

1 👤 Paraphrase or ask learners to read the information in the box. They read the interview title and try to write three pieces of information or opinions that they think will be in the text. Check some ideas with the class, but do not tell them whether they are right or wrong as the aim is for them to predict what will be in the text.

2 👥 Learners discuss the questions in pairs. Do not do feedback on their answers at the moment.

3 👤👥 Learners read the interview and decide whether their predictions for Exercises 1 and 2 above were right. They compare with a partner. Check answers with the class.

> **Answers to Exercise 2**
>
> 1 Yes, it has.
> 2 People are living longer in most regions.
> 3 Old people may be unable to care for themselves for health reasons.
> 4 If old people are retired and not paying taxes but still need healthcare this could put a strain on social systems.
> 5 Benefits could be that less money is needed for education. Older people may have saved money to spend on themselves and their familes and may give time to voluntary organizations, or be able to help care for younger family members.

WHILE READING

READING FOR DETAIL

4 👤👥 Learners read the statements and decide if they are *true*, *false* or it *does not say*. Point out that *Thus far* in Question 5 means *until now*. They complete the exercise. Learners compare answers, saying what is wrong with the false statements. Check answers with the class.

Answers

1 DNS 2 T 3 F (In many countries, an increasing number of older people are living by themselves, often without any relatives living nearby.) 4 T
5 F (Supermarkets have responded by providing more home delivery services and there has been a significant growth in companies providing services that would have traditionally been done by family members.) 6 F (In countries where the percentage of children and young people is lower, there are fewer costs in the education system.) 7 DNS 8 T

2 👥 Focus learners on the sentences. Do an example together, reminding learners that they can use a maximum of three words to complete the gaps. They complete the exercise. Learners check answers in pairs. Check answers with the class.

Answers

1 look after themselves
2 social activities
3 private nursing care
4 economic impact
5 savings, free time
6 voluntary

READING BETWEEN THE LINES

MAKING INFERENCES FROM THE TEXT

6 👥👥 Learners work in pairs suggesting reasons for statements in the text. They should use logic and their own knowledge. Remind them that they are only giving their opinions in this section. Learners compare with another pair. Check answers with the class.

Possible answers

1 Because of scientific advances, healthier diets and less poverty in many places.
2 People are more mobile nowadays; they often have to move away from their families to find jobs.
3 People are busier these days and maybe lazier too!
4 As older people are living longer, there may not be enough houses or apartments available for younger people. They may also be very expensive.
5 They may have been saving for a long time. They do not have to spend so much money on their children, who are now adults.
6 Older people can study at their own pace. They can also study subjects they are interested in rather than ones they need for a job.

DISCUSSION

7 👥👥👥 Learners discuss the questions. Monitor to help with vocabulary and to encourage participation. Check a few answers with the class. Encourage learners to respond to each other's ideas.

Answers will vary.

READING 2

PREPARING TO READ

> ### Optional activity
>
> Focus learners on the photo. Ask if they can guess which country the picture is from (Saudi Arabia). Ask learners if they can guess what it will be about, based on the picture (the unusually young population of the country).

1 👥👥👥 Remind learners of the topic of Reading 1 (the problems, impact and solutions related to an ageing population). Learners discuss in pairs what the effects of a young population could be on a country. If they need more guidance, suggest they focus on education, housing and the economy. Learners share their ideas with another pair. Check some ideas with the class.

UNDERSTANDING KEY VOCABULARY

2 👤👥 Point out to learners that a population pyramid is a type of graph which shows the different ages of a population. Ask them what they think *bottom heavy* means in Question 1. They choose a, b or c (the answer is c). Learners continue the exercise, using a dictionary if necessary. Learners compare answers with a partner. Check answers with the class.

Answers

1 c 2 b If the following are the ages of some children: 3, 6, 6, 6, 7, 9 11, 11, 13, the *median age* is 7, because it is in the middle. 3 b 4 a

WHILE READING

READING FOR MAIN IDEAS

3 👤👥 Learners read the text and see how many of their ideas from Exercise 1 were mentioned. They compare answers with the partner they discussed the topic with. Check a few answers with the class.

READING FOR DETAIL

4 👤👥 Learners read the sentences and refer back to the text for the words or numbers they need to complete them. They may need to do some calculations for this. Learners compare with a partner. Check answers with the class.

> **Answers**
>
> 1 young 2 five 3 57 4 20 5 less/lower 6 one
> 7 sectors 8 expansion

READING BETWEEN THE LINES

WORKING OUT MEANING FROM CONTEXT

5 👤👥 Allow learners time to find the words and phrases in the text and think about what they mean. They should not use dictionaries but look at the context and any clues within the word or phrase itself. They discuss the meanings in pairs. Check answers with the class.

> **Answers**
>
> 1 already been written about widely 2 a description of a certain population 3 looking carefully at something 4 Gross Domestic Product – how much a country earns from the goods it produces and services it offers 5 problem 6 because of this
> 7 money to be used for something

DISCUSSION

6 👥👥👥 Learners discuss the questions. Monitor to help with vocabulary and to encourage participation. Check a few answers with the class. Encourage learners to respond to each other's ideas.

> Answers will vary.

◉ LANGUAGE DEVELOPMENT

RETIREMENT AND THE ELDERLY

1 👤👥 Learners chose a word from the box to make each set of collocations and phrases. Elicit which word could be used in all the examples in the first set (*retirement*). Make sure that learners understand that in the first

four examples, retirement is the final word and in the last two examples it is the first word. Learners complete the exercise, using a dictionary if necessary. They check with a partner, discussing meaning of the words and collocations. Check answers with the class. Learners record useful words.

> **Answers**
>
> 1 retirement 2 pension 3 health 4 age 5 memory
> 6 years

2 👤👥 Learners complete the sentences using collocations and phrases from the previous exercise. In some cases there is more than one possible answer. They check with a partner. Check answers with the class.

> **Answers**
>
> 1 retirement/pension age 2 years of marriage
> 3 pay into/contribute to a pension 4 active retirement
> 5 ill health / old age / memory loss 6 a good memory
> 7 coming years 8 health worker 9 retirement age / pension age

ACADEMIC COLLOCATIONS WITH PREPOSITIONS

3 👤👥 Learners fill in the prepositions in the table, using a dictionary if necessary. They check with a partner. Check answers with the class.

> **Answers**
>
> 1 in 2 of 3 on 4 up 5 with 6 in 7 on 8 in

4 👤👥 Learners complete the sentences with the phrases from the previous exercises. They check with a partner. Check answers with the class.

> **Answers**
>
> 1 rely on 2 In contrast 3 range of 4 focus on
> 5 In brief 6 in theory 7 identify with 8 sum up

CRITICAL THINKING

ANALYZE

1 👤👥 Focus learners on the population graph. Tell them it is similar to a diagram they will be writing about later. Ask the following questions to check learners know how interpret the diagram.

- What's the general topic of this diagram? (The age of the population of Japan.)
- Why is it divided into two colours? (Each colour represents men and women.)
- What does the bottom axis show? (The percentage of men and women.)
- What does the side axis show? (The age ranges represented in the diagram.)
- What information does the graph give? (It tells us what percentage of the male and female population are different ages at a specific point in time.)

Give learners a few minutes to look at the questions and the graph alone and find the answers. They compare answers with a partner. Check answers with the class.

> **Answers**
>
> 1 It is from 2010.
> 2 It was nearly 127 million in 2010.
> 3 There are more over-40s.
> 4 Women live longer.
> 5 About 35% are aged over 60.
> 6 The shape is completely different. Whereas the Saudi Arabian pyramid is bottom heavy, Japan's is more middle and top heavy, indicating an older population.

2 👤👥 Give learners time to look at the two population graphs. Point out that these are predictions for 2050 (establish how many years in the future this is) for Japan and Saudi Arabia. Learners decide which graph relates to Japan and which to Saudi Arabia. They discuss their ideas with a partner, saying why they reached these conclusions. Check answers with the class.

> **Answers**
>
> The first graph is Japan. There is an increased number of older people at the top of the pyramid, and fewer younger people at the bottom compared to the 2010 graph. The average age of the population is between 75–79. The second graph is Saudi Arabia. The population as a whole is older than in 2010, but the average age of the population is still young, between 30–34.

3 👥👥 Learners read the list of problems and discuss in pairs which of those a society may face if they have an elderly population. Before they start, check understanding of *declining fertility* (fewer babies are being born) and

remind learners of the difference between *emigration* (leaving a country) and *immigration* (coming to live in a new country). Learners compare ideas with another pair. Check answers with the class. You may prefer to leave this feedback stage until after Exercise 4, especially with a strong group.

> **Possible answers**
>
> 1 This might be a problem. If people stay in their jobs longer it could mean fewer jobs for young people.
> 2 This might be a problem. If many elderly people live alone, this could mean there are not enough houses for others.
> 3 Yes.
> 4 Yes.
> 5 Probably not.
> 6 This depends on the country. As mentioned in Reading 1, many older people have more savings and disposable income. However, in many countries this is not the case.
> 7 Yes, the fertility rate will probably decline.
> 8 This might be a problem. Taxes may need to be higher to pay pension and healthcare costs.
> 9 Probably not, but young people may feel they will have more opportunities abroad and decide to emigrate.
> 10 This might be a problem. An ageing population may mean there are not enough people to make a full workforce.

APPLY

4 👤👥 Learners use the phrases from Exercise 3 to complete the sentences. They compare answers with a partner. Check answers with the class.

> **Answers**
>
> 1 Increased healthcare costs
> 2 youth unemployment
> 3 Higher taxes
> 4 high pension costs
> 5 declining fertility
> 6 increased immigration

UNDERSTAND

5 👥 Focus learners on the statements. After reading them, they discuss the importance of each one in pairs and try to agree on an order of priority. Assure them that there are no right or wrong answers. Check some ideas with the class.

> **Answers will vary.**

WRITING

GRAMMAR FOR WRITING

NUMERICAL WORDS AND PHRASES

1 👤👥 Paraphrase or ask learners to read the information in the box. Focus learners on the pie chart before they look at Exercise 1. Ask the following questions:

- What does the chart show? (The total population of Japan divided into the proportion of people who are children, adults of working age and those over 65.)
- Can you make any generalizations about the information about the elderly? (About or just under a quarter of the population are elderly.)
- Why might it be more effective to write a generalization for this type of information rather than give precise figures? (It is easier to read and relate to, readers can look at the graph more closely if they want precise information.)
- How does the number of children compare to the number of elderly people? (They represent just over half of the population.)
- What adjectives could you use to express the large difference between the working age population and the elderly? (*significant*, *sizable*, *overwhelming*, *huge*, *great*)

Learners complete the sentences, referring to the pie chart and using a dictionary if necessary. They compare with a partner. Check answers with the class.

> **Answers**
>
> 1 majority 2 minority 3 times 4 proportion 5 double
> 6 triple 7 half 8 quarter

LANGUAGE OF PREDICTIONS

2 👤👥 Paraphrase or ask learners to read the information in the box. Remind them that when you make a prediction, you do not know something for certain, but you use information you have available to guess. So if a chart shows that sales have been rising steadily and you see no reason for that to change, then you can *predict* that sales will continue to rise. Ask learners what kind of words we use when we make predictions. (modal verbs such as *may*, *might*, *could*, *likely*, *possible*, *probably*, etc.)

Learners match the sentence halves. Remind them to look at the grammar of the sentence as well as the vocabulary to find the answer. They compare with a partner. Check answers with the class. Ask learners to highlight the words that express a prediction as well as any other words that show how they are used in a sentence (see below).

> **Answers**
>
> 1 b (is likely to be) 2 a (may well be) 3 e (is expected to)
> 4 d (is set to) 5 g (are unlikely to) 6 c (is projected to)
> 7 f (are predicted to)

3 👤 Learners use the language from Exercise 2 to make the sentences into predictions. Point out that they must use the word in brackets in their answers. Do the first one together as an example. Learners check with a partner. Check answers with the class.

> **Possible answers**
>
> 1 The population is likely to increase in the future.
> 2 Oil prices may well come down this year.
> 3 Unemployment is predicted to remain at the same level in the coming months.
> 4 The cost of living is set to rise over the decade.
> 5 There is expected to be more competition for university places in the future. (or) More competition for university places is expected in the future.
> 6 There is unlikely to be a reduction in the number of schools. (or) A reduction in the number of schools is unlikely.
> 7 Salaries are projected to rise because of access to better training and education.

ACADEMIC WRITING SKILLS

INTERPRETING GRAPHS AND CHARTS

1 👤👥 Ask learners what the difference is between *describing* a graph and *interpreting* one. (When you *describe* you only say what you see. When you *interpret* you explain the information and often use it to make points or predictions.) Focus learners on the writing task (which is similar to the final one for this unit). Then they read the statements and say whether they are true or false for this task. Learners compare with a partner. Check answers with the class.

Answers

1 F (You should be selective and only use the most interesting points.)
2 T (You can use phrases such as 'just over half', 'three times as many', etc.)
3 F (No. In an examination, you will lose marks for copying the question. It is better to paraphrase instead, but it is acceptable to use the same key words.)
4 T (Remember to use language of comparison when doing this.)
5 T (This can be an effective strategy and lead to interesting conclusions but note that while some type of diagrams only require comparison and others only require description of trends, this one has both.)
6 F (In this task you need a short introduction saying what the graph relates to and the aim of your essay. You can conclude with the main noticeable trends or effects.)
7 F (The essay should use formal academic language with no contractions.)
8 T (In this task you are asked to predict based on the information. However, this is not always the case. In the IELTS writing test (Task 1) for example, you are only asked to describe information. Read the task prompt carefully.)

2 🔳 Learners look at the writing task, the charts and the five sentences and decide which sentences they would include in the essay. Learners compare with a partner. Check answers with the class.

Answers

1 No. Too many figures make this difficult to read, it would be better to use more generalizations instead.
2 No. This is too informal and uses personal pronouns (I), colloquial language (be really tough, cos) and contractions (it'll, there'll).
3 Yes.
4 No. This repeats the words of the title, so needs paraphrasing.
5 Yes.

WRITING TASK

WRITING A FIRST DRAFT

1 🔳 Focus learners on the three population pyramids and the writing task title. Check they understand it fully by asking the following questions:

- What kind of academic writing task is it? (An essay describing population data and its implications.)
- Should you add any information that is not in the graphs? (No, but you can add predictions based on the information.)

- Is Reading 1 or 2 in this unit most closely related to the style and structure of your writing task? (Reading 2, an essay which describes a population pyramid and makes predictions based on the information in it.)

Learners look back at Reading 2 and number the paragraph descriptions. With a weaker group, learners compare with a partner. Otherwise quickly check answers with the class.

Answers

a 2 b 4 c 3 d 6 e 5 f 1

2 🔳🔳 Learners write a sentence about the general picture of what the graphs represent. This is a good opportunity for learners to practise paraphrasing essay titles. Monitor closely to check that they are giving enough information but using different words from the title. Learners compare sentences with their partner and help each other to improve them. Check some sentences with the class.

Suggested answer

The three graphs indicate the changes in age of the world population over the past 65 years and predict how this may change further by the year 2100.

3 🔳 Learners study the graphs carefully and choose three of the most interesting developments or predictions to write about. They need to remember that they will be using this information to write about the global impact if the 2100 figures were correct, so they need to focus mainly on the 2010 and 2100 charts.

4 🔳 Learners sum up what they feel is the most interesting or noticeable trend in the graph. It may be a good idea for learners to compare ideas here.

5 🔳 For the final three paragraphs learners need to write predictions of how the age of the global population may affect the world in the future. To do this, they look at the implications that were mentioned in Reading 2 on page 184. Learners then try to write three implications for their writing task. Give learners the opportunity to ask you questions about vocabulary or use dictionaries. Tell them they will not be allowed to use dictionaries while they are writing.

6 👤 Learners write the essay. Allow about 40 minutes for this. They should write at least 250 words and highlight any language (including spelling) of which they are unsure. Give them a warning five minutes before the end of the set time.

EDIT

7 👤 To encourage learners to take responsibility for their own learning, tell them to check their writing using the task checklist. Stress that this is a very important part of the writing process as it helps learners to learn from their mistakes. Encourage them to look back over their plan and at the unit.

8 👤 Learners make any necessary changes to their essays.

9 👤 Learners check their written language now using the language checklist. They can also check any spelling that they were unsure of by looking back over the unit, using a dictionary, or by asking other learners or you. In addition, remind them to check carefully for any errors that they often make in their writing (e.g. particular spellings, subject-verb agreements, omitting verbs, etc.)

10 👤👥 Learners make any other changes and write up their final essays. If comfortable doing so, they can read each other's writing and suggest improvements before handing the essays in to you for marking.

OBJECTIVES REVIEW

See Introduction, page 9 for ideas about using the Objectives review with your learners.

WORDLIST

See Introduction, page 9 for ideas about how to make the most of the Wordlist with your learners.

REVIEW TEST

See page 122 for the photocopiable Review test for this unit and page 92 for ideas about when and how to administer the Review test.

MODEL ANSWER

See page 134 for the photocopiable Model answer.

RESEARCH PROJECT

Produce a podcast which explores the elderly's concerns for the future.

Divide the class into groups. Explain that they will be producing a podcast on the elderly. Ask them to interview elderly relatives about their concerns for the future. They could ask them how things have changed, where the world is heading, health, the home, travel, and how the country has changed in their lifetime.

The group thinks of the questions for the interview and each learner asks their relatives, before bringing them together their answers as a group to create and broadcast the podcast.

REVIEW TESTS

The *Review tests* are designed to be used after the learners have completed each unit of the Student's book. Each *Review test* checks learners' knowledge of the key language areas taught in the unit and practices the reading skills from the unit. The *Review tests* take 50 minutes to complete but you may wish to adjust this time depending on your class or how much of the Student's book unit you covered. *Review tests* can be given as homework as general revision. Photocopy one test for each learner. Learners should do the tests on their own. You can check the answers by giving learners their peers' papers to mark or correct the papers yourself. Keep a record of the results to help monitor individual learner progress.

REVIEW TEST 1 ANSWERS

Reading
1 1C 2D 3B 4E 5A
2 1F 2T 3T 4T 5F

Vocabulary
3 1 food miles 2 insist 3 freshness 4 authentic
   5 perfectionist 6 consumption 7 selling point
   8 situated 9 farms 10 discount

Language development
4 1 increased 2 removed 3 confuse 4 exhausted
   5 exclude
5 1 diet 2 Obesity 3 outlets 4 monopoly 5 poverty

Grammar for writing
6 1 products 2 life 3 site 4 city 5 change
7 1 Around ~~ago ten years~~ ten years ago, I was living in Tokyo.
   2 Correct
   3 At the present time, the economy seems to be doing well.
   4 ~~Historic~~, Historically Canada has always been a multilingual country.
   5 More and more people have travelled abroad in ~~recently~~ recent years.
   6 Correct
   7 Correct
   8 International communication was very slow in ~~a~~ the past, before the internet.

Academic writing skills
8 1c 2d 3a 4b
9 1a 2c 3b 4c 5a 6b

REVIEW TEST 2 ANSWERS

Reading
1 1B 2A 3C 4E 5D
2 1T 2T 3F 4T 5DNS

Vocabulary
3 1 distance learning 2 face-to-face 3 virtual 4 tuition
   5 tutorials 6 lecture 7 modules 8 academic
   9 vocational 10 scholarships

Language development
4 1 assignments 2 journals 3 examination 4 plagiarism
   5 semesters 6 motivation 7 aspect 8 dissertation
   9 components 10 core

Grammar for writing
5 1 contrast 2 difference 3 Similarly 4 Unlike 5 whereas
   6 Like 7 different in that 8 similarity 9 the same way
   10 Conversely

Academic writing skills
6 a3 b5 c1 d2 e4
7 1b 2d 3a 4c 5e

REVIEW TEST 3 ANSWERS

Reading
1 1C 2B 3E 4D 5A
2 1a 2b 3a 4b 5c

Vocabulary
3 1 Alternative 2 fund 3 patient 4 proponent 5 evidence
   6 treatment 7 remedy 8 practitioner 9 therapy
   10 Natural

Language development
4 1 epidemic 2 sedentary 3 preventable 4 cosmetic
   5 drug
5 1b 2c 3b 4a 5a

Grammar for writing
6 1 I went to the pharmacy to pick up **the** antibiotics which my doctor had prescribed me.
   2 One of **the** biggest problems with doctors is that they are often too busy to spend time listening to people.
   3 I have **an** appointment at the clinic next week – I hope it will be OK.
4 I am having surgery on my foot next week – and after that, I will have **a** short holiday from work.
5 Most governments recognize that obesity is **a** growing problem.

Academic writing skills
7 1 Despite the 2 Nevertheless 3 spite 4 Despite 5 Even though
8 Sentences 2, 5 and 10
9 a9 b6 c3 d4 e1 f7 g8

REVIEW TEST 4 ANSWERS

Reading

1 The text answers questions 1, 3, 4, 6 and 8

2 1T 2DNS 3F 4F 5DNS

Vocabulary

3 1 compulsory 2 prohibit 3 regulations 4 liable
5 responsibility 6 legislation 7 action 8 play it safe
9 banned 10 trial and error

Language development

4 **allow:** authorize permit legalize; **curb:** limit restrict;
ban: prohibit criminalize

5 1d 2c 3a 4b 5e

Grammar for writing

6 1 means 2 Because of 3 Consequently 4 a result of

7 1 Provided that you are well prepared, it is acceptable
to take risks.

2 As long as you don't put other people in danger,
most risks are fine.

3 You can use the car on condition that you bring it
back safely.

Academic writing skills

8 1E 2C 3B 4D 5A

9 1B 2A 3E 4D 5C

REVIEW TEST 5 ANSWERS

Reading

1 1E 2C 3B 4A 5D

2 1 DNS 2T 3F 4DNS 5T

Vocabulary

3 1 products 2 dry 3 roast 4 mould 5 shell 6 harvest
7 melt 8 package 9 grind 10 manufacturer

Language development

4 1 cultivated 2 consult with 3 distributing 4 emerged
5 extracted

5 1b 2c 3c 4a 5a

Grammar for writing

6 1 Before the paper is sold on rolls, it is cut to the
correct length by a machine.

2 Before the chocolate is taken out of the mould,
make sure it is completely cool.

3 After the coffee has been ground, use it
immediately.

4 Before the product is distributed, it is checked very
carefully.

5 After the tea leaves have been picked, they are
taken to the factory.

Academic writing skills

7 1d 2a 3b 4e 5c

8 1b 2d 3e 4a 5c

REVIEW TEST 6 ANSWERS

Reading

1 1C 2D 3A 4E 5B

2 1c 2g 3f 4d 5a

Vocabulary

3 1 major 2 severe 3 large-scale 4 dams 5 disaster
6 barriers 7 hurricanes 8 seasonal 9 devastating
10 long-term

Language development

4 1 a government report 2 disaster mitigation 3 risk
reduction 4 flood protection 5 product manufacturing
6 risk analysis

5 1a 2a 3c 4b

Grammar for writing

6 1 It is important to prepare for natural disasters.

2 It is surprising that more people didn't know about
the tsunami.

3 It is worth remembering that earthquakes can
happen at any time.

4 It is a good idea to prepare for emergencies.

5 It is a sad fact that many homes were destroyed in
the hurricane.

Academic writing skills

7 b1 a2 e3 d4 c5

8 1c 2b 3e 4a 5d

REVIEW TEST 7 ANSWERS

Reading

1 Opinions which are mentioned: 1, 2, 4, 6, 8

2 1b 2a 3e 4d 5c

Vocabulary

3 1 durable 2 tower 3 install 4 affordable 5 tomb
6 skyscrapers 7 green 8 efficient 9 compromise
10 straw

Language development

4 1 environment 2 functional 3 efficiently 4 depress
5 responsibly 6 architecture

5 1c 2a 3b 4a

Grammar for writing

6 1 critical 2 calculate 3 undoubtedly 4 a great deal
5 Fundamentally 6 justified 7 approximately 8 have a
positive impact on 9 of no benefit to 10 considerable

Academic writing skills

7 1 In spite of this 2 For these 3 This 4 That is why
5 These

8 1b 2f 3g 4h 5a

REVIEW TEST 8 ANSWERS

Reading

1 1B 2A 3D 4C

2 1c 2e 3a 4d 5f 6b

Vocabulary

3 1h 2e 3d 4b 5g 6a 7f 8i 9j 10c

Language development

4 1b 2a 3c 4b 5a

5 1 diminishing 2 instigate 3 contesting 4 consulting 5 utilizes

Grammar for writing

6 1 who 2 which 3 when 4 where 5 whose

7 1 obvious 2 inherent 3 serious 4 distinct 5 apparent

Academic writing skills

8 1 Most **governments** are committed to reducing their carbon footprint.

2 One **of** the most serious problems we face today is the risk of environmental pollution.

3 We need to protect our **environment** for our children.

4 The problem **with** our dependence on oil is that eventually it will run out.

5 Most people **believe** that we should use more alternative fuels.

9 1 We need to book **accommodation** for our holiday next month

2 Correct

3 More **research** has to be conducted before we can make a decision.

4 Correct

5 This computer had a lot of **software** installed.

6 How **much** equipment do we need to take with us?

7 I really appreciate all the **feedback** you gave me.

8 Correct

REVIEW TEST 9 ANSWERS

Reading

1 1C 2A 3D 4B

2 1C 2B 3A 4B 5D 6C

Vocabulary

3 1 fine 2 sculptures 3 aesthetic 4 acknowledge 5 creative 6 calligraphy 7 photography 8 mechanical 9 cynical 10 banal

Language development

4 1 suggested 2 insisted 3 denied 4 argued

5 1 avant-garde 2 monumental 3 lifelike 4 abstract 5 moving 6 expressive

Grammar for writing

6 1c 2h 3g 4i 5e

7 1 not 2 doesn't 3 was 4 it 5 this

Academic writing skills

8 1 These 2 For example 3 items 4 such labels 5 their own 6 In contrast 7 This 8 Although 9 the majority 10 That's why

REVIEW TEST 10 ANSWERS

Reading

1 The text answers questions 1, 3, 4, 7, 8

2 1 1970 2 127 (the population was one million fewer than in 2010) 3 25 4 13 5 2010

Vocabulary

3 1 changes 2 population 3 expectancy 4 impact 5 activities

4 1 workforce 2 elderly 3 shortage 4 decline 5 maintain

Language development

5 1a 2c 3b 4b 5c

6 1 in 2 on 3 with 4 of 5 up

Grammar for writing

7 1 proportion 2 minority 3 majority 4 tripled 5 doubled

8 1 may well decrease 2 are set to rise 3 is projected to rise 4 are unlikely to be 5 are expected to be

Academic writing skills

9 1 diagram 2 shows 3 analysis 4 steadily 5 consequences 6 impact

10 1C 2B 3A 4D

Name: .... **Date:** ....

READING (10 marks)

1 Read the article about English-language signs around the world. Match the descriptions (1–5) to the correct paragraph (A–E). 1 mark for each correct answer.

   1 The signs sometimes use incorrect English. _____

   2 An explanation of why English is on signs everywhere. _____

   3 These signs are not for tourists. _____

   4 English is not taking over other languages. _____

   5 Introducing the topic. _____

A English is one of the most well-known languages in the world. You can see it on signs everywhere, not only in English-speaking countries such as the UK. If you look around the streets of Tokyo, for example, you will find that Japanese is the most common language on signs. However, the second-most visible language is English. According to some studies, around 20% of signs in Tokyo are in English. Of course, there is no large native-English population in Tokyo, but other studies have found similar patterns all over the world. So who are these signs for?

B Most people agree that English signs in other countries are not for the benefit of tourists. In Dubai, for example, English is visible in cafés, shops and on adverts. However, only a very small number of foreigners in Dubai are from English-speaking countries, compared with people from countries like India or Sri Lanka.

C Many researchers now believe that English signs are not intended for English speakers. In fact, they are 'speaking' to the local population. In Tokyo, for example, an English-language sign may include mistakes or may use English in a strange way. However, this is not important, because these signs are 'speaking' to a Japanese audience.

D One possible reason for this is that English is currently exotic and fashionable for many people. If English stops being fashionable, then these signs will probably disappear very quickly. In the same way, if you walk around London, you will find many cafés with Italian-language signs. These signs may not make sense to an Italian person, but that is not important. The signs are 'speaking' to people in London who think that Italian is something fashionable.

E At the same time, many researchers believe that English is not replacing other languages culturally. For example, if there are a large number of English-language signs in a place like Tokyo, this does not mean that British or American culture is replacing Japanese. On the contrary, it shows that the Japanese language is strong, and the Japanese can allow another language to be publically visible at the same time as their own.

---

2 Read the article again. Are the statements below true (T) or false (F)? 1 mark for each correct answer.

   1 The most visible language in Tokyo is English. _____

   2 According to the article, these English-language signs are for the local population. _____

   3 Some English-language signs in Tokyo contain language which might confuse English people. _____

   4 In London, many people have a positive attitude to Italian-language signs. _____

   5 The Japanese language is quickly dying out in Tokyo. _____

VOCABULARY (10 marks)

3 Complete the text with the words in the box. 1 mark for each correct answer.

authentic   food miles   perfectionist   freshness   farms   situated   insist   discount   selling point   consumption

A big social question at the moment is: Is it OK to eat something which was grown in a faraway country? People often talk about [1] _____ – how far fruit or meat has travelled before we buy it. Most people will [2] _____ that the more food has travelled, the worse it is. Not only is it bad for the environment, but by the time it gets to us, it will have lost all its [3] _____ . Many also argue that eating only local food is more [4] _____, as this is how we naturally should eat. A true local food [5] _____ will tell you that eating exotic fruit in winter is just wrong.

The problem is, of course, that our [6] _____ habits have changed. We are used to eating what we want, when we want it. Many of us like to eat foreign food. The main [7] _____ of a beautiful piece of French cheese is that it was made in France – not in a factory [8] _____ 20 miles away.

Another argument is that eating food from distant lands may actually be *better* for the environment. Yes, flying lamb from New Zealand is expensive and isn't great for the environment. However, the reason we buy lamb from [9] _____ in New Zealand is because it's cheaper to raise sheep in that country. That's why lamb from New Zealand is often sold at a bigger [10] _____ than local meat.

LANGUAGE DEVELOPMENT (10 marks)

4 Choose the correct verb in each sentence. Use the phrasal verbs in brackets to help you. 1 mark for each correct answer.

1 The number of people going abroad to find work has *continued / increased* in recent years. (go up)

2 When the new government came into power, they *removed / excluded* many of the old street signs and put up new ones. (take away)

3 My parents both speak different languages. I'm bilingual, but when I speak to them, I sometimes *confuse / separate* one word with another. (mix up)

4 Some people predict that oil supplies will be *refused / exhausted* in a few decades. (use up)

5 We cannot *exclude / separate* the possibility that Chinese will become the world's number one language. (leave out)

5 Complete the gaps with the words in the box. You will not need to use all the words. 1 mark for each correct answer.

obesity   diet   monopoly   outlets   supermarkets   consumption   poverty   multinational

1 Becoming overweight is often a consequence of a _____ which is too high in fat.

2 _____ is a growing health problem for many people in richer countries.

3 Many retail _____ have closed down recently because of the economic crisis.

4 In this country, there is only one train company, so it has a _____ in the travel business.

5 We must do something to help the millions of people who are living in _____.

GRAMMAR FOR WRITING (10 marks)

6 Complete the noun phrases in the sentences below with the head nouns in the box. There are four nouns you do not need. 1 mark for each correct answer.

> products transport site figure change people city life cuisine

1 There are a range of _____ in supermarkets now which our grandparents could not buy.
2 The internet has become a part of modern _____.
3 I only use one social-networking _____ – I haven't got time to use all of them.
4 Tokyo is a major world _____ and its population is set to grow in the next few decades.
5 A recent _____ is the amount of people who use a car to travel to work.

7 Five of the sentences below contain a mistake. Find the mistakes and correct them. 1 mark for each correct answer.

1 Around ago ten years, I was living in Tokyo.
2 There are more supermarkets in the city centre these days.
3 At present time, the economy seems to be doing well.
4 Historic, Canada has always been a multilingual country.
5 More and more people have travelled abroad in recently years.
6 Nowadays, it is common to learn a second language.
7 Thai food is currently becoming very popular around the world.
8 International communication was very slow in a past, before the internet.

ACADEMIC WRITING SKILLS (10 marks)

8 Read sentences 1–4 from different essay introductions and match them to types of essay (a–d). 1 mark for each correct answer.

1 I will discuss the issue of growing poverty in our country. I will also go on to recommend ways in which we can deal with this situation. _____
2 I will explore the popularity of ready meals, and try to explain how they became so common. _____
3 Fast food is not, as many people claim, an unhealthy product. This essay will argue that fast food, if eaten as part of a balanced diet, has no negative effects on children. _____
4 I will first outline the advantages of a vegetarian diet, then discuss its disadvantages. _____

   a Defending an argument   c Problem – solution
   b For and against   d Cause and effect

9 Match the sentences (1–6) to the parts of an essay in which they would be found (a–c). 1 mark for each correct answer.

1 This essay explores the changing consumer habits of people in London. _____
2 To summarize, this is not a recent problem, and there is no easy solution. _____
3 Another reason, which I will now discuss, is that people are not educated about healthy foods. _____
4 I would like to conclude this essay by mentioning a recent development in consumer habits. _____
5 In this essay, I will discuss the growing problem of obesity in this country. _____
6 I will now turn to the ways that advertising has affected people's attitudes. _____

   a Introduction
   b Body paragraph
   c Conclusion

TOTAL ___/50

Name: ....   **Date:** ....

READING (10 marks)

1 Read the article about the value of education. Match the descriptions (1–5) to the correct paragraph (A–E). 1 mark for each correct answer.

   1 an example of how university education is not necessary for success _____

   2 an overview of the main topics being discussed _____

   3 the important personal qualities needed in a job _____

   4 a general summary and conclusion _____

   5 the benefits of education _____

A Do schools really prepare young people for real life? There are many examples of successful people who never went to university. Similarly, are employers these days really looking for people with qualifications in subjects like History or Literature? Research seems to indicate that what employers really want are people with experience which isn't traditionally part of a school or university curriculum.

B To illustrate one side of the argument, we can look at the example of an entrepreneur from London who is the director of a large electronics company. He left school at the age of 16, after having failed his exams and his first job was helping out with his parents' small cleaning business. After a few weeks, he had saved £100. With this, he started to buy small electrical goods, which he then sold at a profit at the local market. He now has an estimated fortune of £70 million, which he made entirely by himself.

C Examples like this show us that there are many valuable skills which we can learn outside the classroom. The ability to work hard and be self-disciplined is arguably more important than learning facts or memorizing poems. Regardless of whether or not you have a degree, companies increasingly want employees with good communication skills, or 'soft skills', as well as qualifications, Of course, these are qualities which can be learnt through experience in the real world.

D However, schools do have an important role in preparing students for the world. As children spend time with other people in school, they learn how to interact in society and to respect rules and authority. As we progress into higher education, we learn how to manage our time and how to deal with deadlines. We learn how to become independent and critical thinkers, how to express our opinion, and how to deal with complicated ideas. In summary, education is not only about facts and figures – it's also about developing important personal qualities.

E In short, we should remember that few of us will become millionaires by selling electronics without an education. Therefore, it is probable that schools do prepare us for the 'real world', because they give the majority of us the necessary tools to fit into society, and allow more people to achieve success without relying on luck.

---

2 Read the article again. Are the statements below true (T), false (F) or the article does not say (DNS)? 1 mark for each correct answer.

   1 The London entrepreneur couldn't go to university. _____

   2 We can learn many important life skills outside of school or university. _____

   3 Employers do not want to hire people with qualifications any more. _____

   4 'Soft skills' are personal qualities which enable someone to work well with other people.

      _____

   5 Most millionaires do not go to university. _____

VOCABULARY (10 marks)

3 Complete the texts below with the words and phrases in the box. 1 mark for each correct answer.

> academic   lecture   vocational   tuition   face-to-face   modules
> distance learning   scholarships   tutorials   virtual

Many people, especially those who already work or have children, are choosing to take
¹ _____ courses. These can be taken anywhere, as long as you have access to a computer
with an internet connection. Students taking these courses do not have ² _____ seminars,
which means that they don't personally meet their lecturers or fellow students. Instead, they have
access to a ³ _____ university which exists almost entirely online.

Because ⁴ _____ fees are rising, it is important to make the most of your time at university.
Don't be afraid to arrange time to have ⁵ _____ where you can discuss any problems or
questions you have with your tutors. Make sure you go to every ⁶ _____ – even ones which
take place early in the morning – and take notes. Finally, make sure you choose the right
⁷ _____. There is nothing worse than being on a course that you are not really interested in.

This college has a range of courses, from traditional ⁸ _____ subjects such as History to
⁹ _____ courses where you can get practical experience of hairdressing or professional
cookery. If you need help with funding, there are many ¹⁰ _____ you can apply for.

LANGUAGE DEVELOPMENT (10 marks)

4 Choose the correct verb in each sentence. 1 mark for each correct answer.

1 In this first module, you will have two *assignments/dissertations* of 1,000 words which you have to hand in before 31 May.

2 When you join our university, you will have access to a wide range of academic *plagiarism/journals* online.

3 There will be an oral *aspect/examination* at the end of the course, and you will need to get a score of over 65% to pass.

4 The student was found guilty of *plagiarism/examination* when it was found that most of his work was copied from others.

5 There are two *journals/semesters*: one in the spring and one in the autumn. You will complete three modules in each one.

6 It is important to keep up your *motivation/assignment* when you are doing a distance-learning course – it is easy to get tired or lazy.

7 Meeting other students is an enjoyable *component/aspect* of being at university.

8 In the last part of your Master's course, you will have to write a *dissertation/journal* of between 15,000–20,000 words.

9 The taught *examination/components* of this course include weekly lectures and seminars.

10 On this course, there are three *examination/core* modules which you must take, and three optional modules which you can choose from.

GRAMMAR FOR WRITING (10 marks)

5 Complete the sentences below with the comparison and contrast language in the box. 1 mark for each correct answer.

> similarly   the same way   conversely   unlike   similarity   whereas   like   contrast   difference   different in that

1 My brother did a PhD in microbiology. In _____, I left school and started work when I was 18.

2 The main _____ between face-to-face courses and online courses is the amount of interaction you have with other people.

3 I have to spend a lot of time in lectures. _____, I have a lot of seminars every week.

4 _____ lectures, you are allowed to ask questions and discuss things in a seminar.

5 I'm studying Mathematics, _____ my friend is studying Literature.

6 _____ my last examination, my assignment made me feel very stressed, especially near the deadline. I hated both of them.

7 Journals and books are _____ journals are collections of articles by several people and are published several times a year.

8 The main _____ between dissertations and assignments is that they are both examples of your own written work.

9 I hated examinations when I was a student. In _____, I try to avoid any kind of test now that I'm older.

10 University was free when I was a student. _____, students nowadays have to pay high tuition fees.

ACADEMIC WRITING SKILLS (10 marks)

6 Put the sentences (a–e) in order to make an essay introduction. 1 mark for each correct answer.

a However this essay will describe the benefits of distance learning as well as why it may actually be more effective than face-to-face learning. _____

b Finally, I will outline my view that face-to-face learning develops many important skills, such as independence and self-motivation. _____

c It is often believed that online distance learning is not as effective as face-to-face study. _____

d For example, distance learning mostly involves working at home alone, whereas face-to-face learning provides a great deal of interaction with teachers and other students. _____

e Firstly, I will report on some research which has been done on students who take online courses, before going on to discuss the advantages and disadvantages of this mode of study. _____

7 Look at the essay task below. Then match the introduction sentences (1–5) to problems (a–e). 1 mark for each correct answer.

Discuss the differences between distance learning and face-to-face learning. In what ways may one of these modes of learning be better than the other?

1 In this essay, I will discuss the differences between distance learning and face-to-face learning, and I will say how one of these modes of learning may be better. _____

2 In this essay, I will discuss distance learning, which has been increasing recently, and I will explain why it is so successful. _____

3 In this essay, I will describe a distance-learning course I took last year, and why I found it to be a very difficult experience. _____

4 In this essay, I will describe why so many people are taking university courses, and which subjects are the most popular. _____

5 Distance learning can be difficult for many people, compared to face-to-face learning. _____

    a This is too personal.

    b This not in the writer's own words.

    c This is not focused on the essay question.

    d This does not address all the parts of the essay question.

    e This does not give the aim of the essay.

TOTAL ___/50

Name: .... **Date:** ....

READING (10 marks)

1 Read the news article about the use of antibiotics. Match the descriptions (1–5) to the correct paragraph (A–E). 1 mark for each correct answer.

1 explaining the cause of the problem _____

2 defining antibiotics _____

3 a possible future situation _____

4 explaining the consequences of the problem _____

5 introducing the problem _____

A According to a recent government report, one of the biggest dangers currently facing the world is neither war nor food shortages. It is in fact the growth in drug-resistant bacteria caused by the overuse of antibiotics, which according to many researchers, could become a catastrophic global threat in the near future.

B Antibiotics are a medicine that destroys harmful bacteria in the body. Alexander Fleming was the first scientist to conduct research into antibiotics when he discovered penicillin in 1929. Since 1945, antibiotics have been widely used in the fight against potentially fatal infections, and this medicine has helped countless people around the world.

C However, according to many researchers, antibiotics are now being overused. Doctors often prescribe them to patients, whether or not they really need them. In addition, farmers routinely mix antibiotics with animal food in the belief that this keeps their livestock healthy, and maximizes profits. These antibiotics eventually find their way into the human food supply as well.

D The problem is that every time a patient takes antibiotics or humans eat meat from animals that have been given food containing them, some bacteria are destroyed, but some also remain. These surviving bacteria can quickly grow and multiply. As many types of bacteria are now overexposed to antibiotics, they become stronger. In other words, the more we use antibiotics, the more bacteria evolve and become resistant to modern drugs.

E New forms of tuberculosis and E-coli infections have recently been observed by doctors in the UK. They warn that highly dangerous forms of these bacterial diseases are becoming increasingly common and that soon they may be much more difficult, or even impossible, to treat. According to some scientists, drug-resistant bacteria could become an even bigger problem for mankind than climate change, unless we stop overusing antibiotics.

2 Read the article again. Choose the best answer (a–c) to complete each sentence. 1 mark for each correct answer.

1 *Drug-resistant bacteria* refers to bacteria which

  a are not affected by medicine.

  b are destroying medicine.

  c cannot fight medicine.

2 Antibiotics have the ability to

  a fight medicine.

  b harm the body.

  c save lives.

3 Antibiotics are

  a not only consumed by patients.

  b used by doctors only when necessary.

  c helping doctors become rich.

4 The overuse of antibiotics is helping
  a to destroy bacteria.
  b bacteria to change and become stronger.
  c patients to become healthier.
5 It is possible that
  a bacteria could cause climate change.
  b doctors will now stop looking for new diseases.
  c diseases will be impossible to treat in the future.

VOCABULARY (10 marks)

3 Choose the best word to complete each sentence. 1 mark for each correct answer.
  1 *Alternative/Conventional* medicine, such as acupuncture, can be used instead of clinical drugs.
  2 Not all doctors believe the government should *fund/debate* homeopathic treatments.
  3 The *patient/doctor* was prescribed antibiotics after the infection got worse.
  4 I am not a *critic/proponent* of homeopathy – I think it is dangerous if someone is seriously ill.
  5 It might be true that we are overusing antibiotics – but we need to see *belief/evidence* of this.
  6 After Abigail was given *consultation/treatment* for her illness, she got better quickly.
  7 If you have a headache, the best *medication/remedy* is to lie down and close your eyes.
  8 Doctor Singh has been a *practitioner/proof* of alternative medicine for 20 years.
  9 She has been going to *therapy/illness* every week since the accident.
  10 *Natural/Synthetic* medicines are usually made from herbs and other plants.

LANGUAGE DEVELOPMENT (10 marks)

4 Complete the sentences with words in the box. 1 mark for each correct answer.

cosmetic drug sedentary preventable epidemic

  1 An _____ is a disease which spreads to a huge number of people in a very short time.
  2 The likelihood of obesity is increased if you have a _____ lifestyle. It is important to make exercise part of your daily routine.
  3 A _____ illness is one which can be avoided by making changes to your lifestyle.
  4 Some people choose to undergo _____ surgery to improve the way they look.
  5 Addiction to sleeping pills is a type of _____ dependency.

5 Choose the best word (a–c) to complete each sentence. 1 mark for each correct answer.
  1 Surgeons need to work with great _____ during an operation.
  2 If you want to work in the _____ profession, you will need to train for several years.
  3 The government has banned this drug – it is now _____.
  4 Nurses often have to work in _____ conditions – in overcrowded hospitals.
  5 People in this country do not have access to _____ health care.

	a	b	c
1	patients	precision	profession
2	medicine	medication	medical
3	alternative	illegal	adverse
4	adverse	adequate	adversity
5	adequate	complex	physical

GRAMMAR FOR WRITING (10 marks)

6 Add the missing article (*a*, *an* or *the*) to each sentence. 1 mark for each correct answer.

1 I went to the pharmacy to pick up antibiotics which my doctor had prescribed me.

2 One of biggest problems with doctors is that they are often far too busy.

3 I have appointment at the clinic next week – I hope it will be OK.

4 I am having surgery on my foot tomorrow – after that, I will have short holiday from work.

5 Most governments recognize that obesity is growing problem.

7 Complete the sentences with language of concession from the box. 1 mark for each correct answer.

| despite   despite the   spite   nevertheless   even though |

1 _____ fact that smoking is very unhealthy, many people find it difficult to give up.

2 I started running three times a week. _____, I am still finding it difficult to lose weight.

3 Some doctors are still prescribing this drug, in _____ of the risks.

4 _____ the government's warning, people are still taking too many antibiotics.

5 _____ I eat healthy food and exercise regularly, I still get colds a few times a year.

ACADEMIC WRITING SKILLS (10 marks)

8 Read the essay question. Then look at the sentences and mark the <u>three</u> which do not belong in an introduction to the essay with a cross. 1 mark for each correct answer.

'Alternative medicine is becoming more widely used. However, many people argue that it should not be used to treat serious illnesses.' Do you agree?

1 The phrase 'alternative' is used because it does not use conventional drugs to treat people. _____

2 In conclusion, this essay has argued that homeopathy should not be used in place of conventional medicine. _____

3 It has been used for thousands of years, but has only recently grown in popularity in the West. _____

4 I would agree that alternative medicines should not be used to treat very serious illnesses. _____

5 In this section, I will discuss the advantages of alternative medicine. _____

6 This essay will discuss the advantages and disadvantages of alternative medicine. _____

7 For this essay, I conducted interviews with several practitioners of alternative medicine, as well as patients. My findings will be presented, along with my own personal opinion. _____

8 I will first give a brief history of alternative medicine. I will then go on to discuss the possible advantages, before listing some of the many disadvantages. _____

9 Alternative medicine has recently become more and more fashionable, with people experimenting with homeopathy and acupuncture as new forms of treatment. _____

10 I will now go on to discuss the results of my research. _____

9 Match the seven correct sentences in the essay introduction to the features (a–g) below. 1 mark for each correct answer.

a a general introduction _____

b the main aim of the essay _____

c limited background information about the subject _____

d an initial response to the question _____

e the definition of the topic _____

f the methods and results of research _____

g the organization of the essay _____

TOTAL ___/50

REVIEW TEST 4

Name: .... **Date:** ....

READING (10 marks)

1 Read the article about why people take risks. Tick the five questions answered in the article. 1 mark for each correct answer.

1 What did Felix Baumgartner achieve?

2 How did Felix Baumgartner prepare for his jump?

3 What do some risk-takers want to prove to other people?

4 What are some of the rewards that risk-takers get?

5 Do men take more risks than women?

6 Why do some people take risks, even though no-one is watching them?

7 What are some of the bad things that happen when risk-taking goes wrong?

8 What happens inside our bodies when we take risks?

In October 2012, the skydiver Felix Baumgartner set a new world record. After sitting inside a tiny capsule at the edge of space, he jumped out when he was 39 kilometres above the Earth. Falling to the ground, he reached a speed of 1,357 kph and broke the sound barrier. This ten-minute jump was extremely well-prepared. Nevertheless, it was a very risky thing to do, and raises the question: Why are some people attracted to dangerous activities?

One reason may be to get attention – Felix Baumgarnter's jump was watched by around 8 million people on YouTube. Some people feel a need to show that they are the fastest or the best at something, and taking public risks is one way to do this. For some competitive individuals (especially in the worlds of sport and business), the financial rewards of taking a risk and achieving what you want can be enormous. Furthermore, if you have taken a risk and won through, then your achievements may be remembered for a very long time. The more thrilling the risk, the bigger the win. Everybody knows who the first person to walk on the Moon or the first team to climb Mount Everest was – but few people know the fifth or ninth people to do so.

However, there are many occasions when people take risks without an audience, for example, in high-risk sports, such as cave diving or mountain climbing. It is clear, then, that there must be other rewards for not playing it safe. One might be the 'adrenaline rush' that people get when they do something dangerous. In frightening situations, the chemical adrenaline is released into our bodies. This makes our hearts beat faster, and helps our bodies if we have to fight or run away. It is possible that this level of excitement might be a reason some people continuously try out exhilarating activities.

In summary, it seems that many people take risks because they dream of success. Of course, there is always the possibility of terrible failure too. At the same time, if everything goes well in a risky activity, then the rewards can be great.

2 Read the article again. Are the statements true (T), false (F) or the article does not say (DNS)? 1 mark for each correct answer.

1 It's possible to get a lot of money if you take a risk and succeed. _____

2 People don't always remember that something can be dangerous. _____

3 People rarely take risks when they are alone. _____

4 Adrenaline makes people want to avoid risk. _____

5 Risk-takers take bigger and more dangerous risks each time they do something. _____

VOCABULARY (10 marks)

3 Choose the best word in each sentence. 1 mark for each correct answer.

1 In most countries, it is *compulsory/responsibility* to wear a seatbelt when you are driving.

2 Some people want to *action/prohibit* the cars in the city centre to make it safer for children.

3 My company has many health and safety *regulations/responsibilities*. For example, you must not pick up heavy boxes by yourself.

4 If you take a risk, then you are *liable/play it safe* if anything goes wrong.

5 When you become a parent, you have a lot of *responsibility/legislation* for your child's happiness.

6 The government is considering new *ban/legislation* to lower the age that you can start driving.

7 We must take *action/liable* to stop the problem before it gets worse.

8 It's better to *trial and error/play it safe* rather than take a risk.

9 After her accident, she was *banned/trial and error* from driving for two years.

10 I didn't know how to solve the problem – it was just a process of *trial and error/play it safe*.

LANGUAGE DEVELOPMENT (10 marks)

4 Put the words in the correct part of the table, according to their meaning. 1 mark for each correct answer.

authorise   limit   permit   prohibit   legalize   restrict   criminalize

allow	curb	ban
authorise	limit	

5 Match the academic nouns (1–5) to their synonyms (a–e). (One mark for each correct answer.)

1 reduction _____   a chaos
2 legislation _____   b unhappiness
3 confusion _____   c law
4 dissatisfaction _____ d fall
5 regulation _____   e rule

GRAMMAR FOR WRITING (10 marks)

6 Complete the sentences with the correct cause and effect language. You will not need to use all the language in the box. 1 mark for each correct answer.

because of   results   consequently   a result of   means   leads

1 It is possible that cars will be banned from the city centre next year. This _____ that people will have to park outside the centre and use public transport more.

2 Research shows that we get an adrenaline rush when we are afraid or stressed. _____ this, the heart begins to beat faster and we are more prepared to fight or run away.

3 He took a risk, but unfortunately it went wrong and he had an accident. _____, he spent two weeks in hospital, and says he will never do anything dangerous again.

4 I took a big risk when I decided to leave my job but as _____ this, I am now working for a better company and earning more money.

7 Rewrite the sentences starting with the word given and using the words in brackets. 2 marks for each correct answer.

1 It is acceptable to take risks if you are well prepared.

Provided _____. (that)

2 Most risks are fine if you don't put other people in danger.

As _____. (long as)

3 You can use the car if you bring it back safely.

You _____. (on the condition that)

ACADEMIC WRITING SKILLS (10 marks)

8 Look at the paragraphs in the essay below. Match the topics (1–5) to each paragraph (A–E). 1 mark for each correct answer.

1 the writer's conclusion _____

2 why exposing children to risk can be harmful _____

3 why exposing children to risk can be positive _____

4 some general characteristics of children _____

5 introducing the essay _____

A _____ I will first give reasons why some parents might let their children experience risk, and what the advantages may be. I will then go on to discuss some of the disadvantages. Finally, I will summarize the arguments and give my own opinion.

B _____ This allows them to experiment and learn things which are useful in later life. For example, if a young child is playing on a sofa and falls off, then they learn the important rule that playing on a sofa is dangerous. This may help them realize how to be careful, and how to realize what is safe and what is not.

C _____ Too much risk is obviously a bad thing if a child becomes hurt or frightened. This can lead to the child developing a phobia or being unable to cope with certain situations. For example, if a child has a bad experience with an aggressive dog when they are young, then this might teach them to be afraid of animals in later life.

D _____ As they develop, they will therefore learn what is dangerous and what is not. Most young children do not really understand the idea of risk and are happy to get into trouble. This means that children are probably natural risk-takers, and this may actually be a valuable way to learn about the world and to experiment.

E _____ After all, one of the roles of the parent is to help and teach their children, so supervised risk is probably very useful for them as they learn the consequences of their actions. Of course, children should not be put in very dangerous situations, but they should certainly be encouraged to try things out. If things sometimes go wrong, for example if they hit their heads, then this could actually be a useful life lesson.

9 Complete the essay with the correct topic sentence number (1–5). 1 mark for each correct answer.

1 Almost all children have a natural curiosity. _____

2 This essay will discuss whether children should be exposed to risk. _____

3 My own opinion is that children should be allowed to experience some risk, but only with the supervision of adults. _____

4 There are certainly some advantages of letting children experience risk. _____

5 There are also disadvantages to letting children be exposed to risk. _____

TOTAL ___/50

REVIEW TEST 5

Name: .... **Date:** ....

READING (10 marks)

1 Read the article about tea production. Match the headings (1–5) to the correct paragraph (A–E). 1 mark for each correct answer.

1 The finished product _____

2 Collecting the tea _____

3 The tea plant _____

4 A much-loved drink _____

5 Creating two forms of tea _____

A	Tea, which is mostly grown in China, India, Sri Lanka and Japan, is popular all over the world. Although most people are aware of where their tea comes from, few understand how it is made.
B	The tea bush (Carmellia sinensis) is much smaller than a tree, at just over one metre high. It is cultivated mainly in subtropical climates at altitudes of over 1,000 metres. Each bush grows for up to 15 years before the leaves are ready to harvest. Even then, only the top leaves are actually used in tea production. Therefore, a lot of bushes are needed to make even a small quantity of tea, and it is not surprising that tea plantations can cover hundreds of kilometres.
C	The tea leaves are always hand-picked to ensure that only the best-quality leaves are taken to the factory. There, they are dried for up to a day. What happens after this process determines the colour of the tea. Perhaps the most well-known forms of the drink are black and green varieties. In fact, there is no difference in the tea leaves at the time they are picked.
D	Black tea is made by allowing the dried leaves to come into contact with the air for another three or four hours. The oxygen reacts with the tea leaves and makes them turn a dark brown. The process is different for making green tea. After drying, the leaves are heated to stop them reacting with oxygen in the air, so that the original green colour does not change. During this process, special ingredients (such as jasmine flowers) might also be added to enhance the flavour of the tea.
E	After this process, most tea is blended (or mixed) with other teas to create the best possible taste. It is then stored or placed in tea bags, ready to be distributed over hundreds or perhaps thousands of kilometres to the person who will eventually add the tea to boiled water.

2 Read the article again. Are the statements below true (T), false (F) or the article does not say (DNS)? 1 mark for each correct answer.

1 China is one of the biggest tea-drinking nations in the world. _____

2 Most of the tea plant is not used. _____

3 All tea is black when it is picked. _____

4 Green tea is healthier than black tea. _____

5 Most of the tea we drink is from lots of different tea plants. _____

VOCABULARY (10 marks)

3 Complete the sentences with the words in the box. 1 mark for each correct answer.

dry harvest mould products package grind shell melt manufacturer roast

1 I drink coffee, but I don't have it with milk. I can't have dairy _____.

2 After the tea leaves have been picked, you need to _____ them for several hours until there is no more water left in them.

3 You _____ the meat by cooking it in an oven for an hour.

4 The liquid chocolate was poured into the _____ and when it became cool and hard, the chocolate was in the shape of a heart.

5 Eggs, nuts and seeds all have a _____,which you break to get the food inside.

6 We had a good _____ this year. The weather was fine, which meant that we were able to grow a lot of food.

7 Chocolate will _____ in a warm place. So don't leave it in your trouser pocket!

8 Chocolates usually come in an attractive _____, such as a large box.

9 You need to _____ the coffee beans into a powder, and then they are ready to add to water.

10 Cadbury's is a famous chocolate _____ which started selling tea, coffee and chocolate in the UK in 1824.

LANGUAGE DEVELOPMENT (10 marks)

4 Write an academic synonym for the verbs in bold. Use the words in the box. 1 mark for each correct answer.

consultwith distributing extracted cultivated emerged

1 Tea is **grown** in the mountains of Sri Lanka and India. _____

2 I had to **talk to** my manager before I was able to make any decision. _____

3 The café was **giving out** free small samples of coffee on the street in an attempt to attract customers. _____

4 New findings about the positive health effects of coffee have **appeared** in the last few years. _____

5 Caffeine can be **removed** from coffee to make a decaffeinated version of the drink. _____

5 Choose the best word (a–c) to complete each sentence. 1 mark for each correct answer.

1 Tea _____ was developed by the Chinese thousands of years ago.

2 The _____ design was not a great success – most people preferred the original.

3 Temperature changes were monitored during the _____ the coffee to France.

4 We are hoping to improve our product _____, so that the customer receives the items more quickly.

5 Coffee _____ is something people can do at home, if they have the right equipment.

1 a cultivated   b cultivation   c cultivate

2 a alter   b altered   c alteration

3 a transport   b transportation   c transportation of

4 a distribution   b distribution of   c distribute

5 a grinding   b grind   c ground

GRAMMAR FOR WRITING (10 marks)

6 Join the sentences together starting with the words given. Use passive structures in each sentence. 2 marks for each correct answer.

1 The machine cuts the paper to the correct length. It is sold on rolls.

Before _____ by a machine.

2 Make sure the chocolate is cool. Take it out of the mould.

Before _____ completely cool.

3 Grind the coffee. Use it immediately.

After _____ immediately.

4 The product is checked very carefully. It is distributed.

Before _____ very carefully.

5 The tea leaves are picked. Then someone takes them to the factory.

After _____ the factory.

ACADEMIC WRITING SKILLS (10 marks)

7 Look at the sentences below. Match the underlined details (1–5) to the descriptions (a–e). 1 mark for each correct answer.

1 Tea, which is mostly grown in China, India, Sri Lanka and Japan, is popular all over the world. _____

2 Tea is cultivated in subtropical climates at altitudes of over 1,000 metres. _____

3 Each bush grows for up to 15 years before it is ready for harvesting. _____

4 After drying, the leaves are heated to stop them reacting with oxygen in the air. _____

5 The tea is hand-picked to ensure that only the best quality leaves are taken to the factory. _____

    a explaining where something happens

    b saying what happens next

    c explaining why something happens

    d giving an extra detail

    e saying what happened earlier

8 Complete the sentences (1–5) with the extra details (a–e). 1 mark for each correct answer.

1 Coffee is grown in many areas _____ .

2 Coffee trees, _____ , take four years to grow.

3 Then, _____ , they are ready to pick.

4 Next, _____ , they are picked by hand.

5 The beans are picked by hand _____ .

    a before the beans are processed

    b including Central America, the Caribbean and Africa.

    c to make sure only the best ones are selected.

    d which are actually fruit trees

    e after the coffee beans turn red

TOTAL ___/50

Name: .... **Date:** ....

READING (10 marks)

1 Read the article about an idea for predicting a tsunami. Match descriptions (1–5) to the correct paragraph (A–E). 1 mark for each correct answer.

1 A more complicated disaster. _____

2 Considering a new early warning system. _____

3 Animals seemed to be aware of what was going to happen. _____

4 No proof is available. _____

5 Animals may have an ability which we cannot yet understand. _____

A When a devastating tsunami hit the island of Sri Lanka in December 2005, **it** caught people by surprise. An earthquake had struck underneath the Indian Ocean, and no-one was able to predict the catastrophe in time. However, according to many witnesses, animals somehow knew what was happening a long time before humans did. Elephants were seeing running away from the sea, and birds such as flamingos were noticeably upset. And at Yala National Park on the southern Sri Lankan coast, very few dead animals were found, despite the park being home to leopards, elephants, bears and hundreds of other large animals.

B **This** has led some people to ask whether animals have some kind of sixth-sense – an ability to understand what is happening without using the traditional senses of sound, sight and so on. It has also led some people to wonder whether animals might be able to provide humans with an early warning that disasters are about to strike.

C Another catastrophic tsunami struck Japan in 2011. It, too, was also an unpredictable event, but **its** large-scale devastation also forced the country to deal with a major environmental disaster, when the Fukushima nuclear plant was hit.

D Although there were no reports of animals running away from the sea before this tsunami, the Japanese city of Susaki has debated whether or not to try out an early-warning system which involves animals. According to various reports, birds such as chickens have been seen getting excited just before large earthquakes. Cats and dogs have also been observed behaving unusually before such events. The mayor of Susaki has thought about asking residents to prepare themselves if **they** notice animals suddenly behaving in a strange way.

E However, as yet, there is no reliable scientific evidence that animals really can sense a disaster is about to strike. **Because of this**, the Japanese government cannot base important decisions on the way some animals might behave.

2 Find the words below (1–5) in the interview. Match them to the ideas they refer to (a–h). You will not need to use all the ideas. 1 mark for each correct answer.

1 it _____   4 they _____

2 this _____   5 Because of this _____

3 its _____

    a It has not been proven that animals know when a tsunami is coming.

    b The park is home to many large animals.

    c a 2005 tsunami which caused a lot of damage

    d residents of Susaki

    e Japan.

    f a second major tsunami

    g Many animals seemed to have known the tsunami was about to occur.

    h People were caught by surprise.

VOCABULARY (10 marks)

3 Complete the texts with words from the boxes. 1 mark for each correct answer.

| large-scale severe major disaster barriers dams |

The River Danube is one of Europe's [1] _____ rivers, and travels through ten different countries. Floods are common along this river, but the flooding of June 2013 was especially [2] _____. After a long period of heavy rain, the river rose by up to two meters and caused [3] _____ damage to several towns. The centre of Passau in Germany was completely underwater for several days, and the flooding destroyed several [4] _____ along the way. Luckily, capital cities such as Vienna, Bratislava and Budapest were safe from [5] _____, because of effective flood [6] _____ built over 100 years ago.

| seasonal hurricanes long-term devastating |

Strong, violent winds known as [7] _____ are common near the Atlantic Ocean. They are [8] _____ and tend to occur between June and November. In October 2012, a [9] _____ storm struck the US, including cities such as New York City and Washington in its path. Several parts of New York were flooded, and the New York Stock Exchange closed for two days. The disaster caused [10] _____ damage to New York State, as more than 100,000 homes were destroyed. In total, the storm created an estimated US $68 billion in damage.

LANGUAGE DEVELOPMENT (10 marks)

4 Complete the table by writing the verb phrases as noun phrases. 1 mark for each correct answer.

1 a report written by the government	_____
2 mitigating a disaster	_____
3 reducing risk	_____
4 protecting against floods	_____
5 manufacturing products	_____
6 analyzing risks	_____

5 Choose the best word (a–c) to complete the collocations. 1 mark for each correct answer.

1 The 2011 Japanese tsunami was a _____ disaster which affected millions of people.

2 Passau, in Germany, experienced _____ flooding when the River Danube burst its banks in 2013.

3 The new dam is _____ project which involves engineers from four different countries.

4 _____ drought has meant that this region has been unable to grow enough food this year.

1 a major	b long-term	c seasonal
2 a severe	b natural	c ambitious
3 a a severe	b a terrible	c an ambitious
4 a Natural	b Prolonged	c Major

GRAMMAR FOR WRITING (10 marks)

6 Complete each sentence using the prompts. 2 marks for each correct answer.

1 important / prepare / natural disasters

It _____

2 surprising / more people didn't know / about the tsunami

It _____

3 worth / remember / earthquakes can happen at any time

It _____

4 good idea / prepare for emergencies

It _____

5 sad fact / many homes were destroyed in the hurricane

It _____

ACADEMIC WRITING SKILLS (10 marks)

7 Put the sentences (a–e) in order to make a paragraph. 1 mark for each correct answer.

a It was caused by an undersea earthquake approximately 70 km out to sea. _____

b In March 2011, Eastern Japan was hit by a major tsunami. _____

c All in all, it was one of the worst disasters ever to hit the country. _____

d This was the fifth-most powerful earthquake ever recorded. _____

e The earthquake caused waves of up to 40 metres to travel 10 km inland and caused large-scale damage. _____

8 Match the functions 1–5 to the sentences (a–e) above. 1 mark for each correct answer.

1 final summary sentence _____

2 topic sentence – introducing what happened _____

3 illustrating what happened with examples _____

4 explanation of why it happened _____

5 further details of the explanation _____

TOTAL ___/50

Name: ....   Date: ....

READING (10 marks)

1 Skim read the article about preserving old buildings. Tick the five opinions mentioned in the article. 1 mark for each correct answer.

   1 Modern Dubai looks nothing like it did in the past. _____

   2 Some tourists enjoy visiting famous skyscrapers. _____

   3 Most Japanese people do not like old styles of architecture. _____

   4 Prague spends a lot of money preserving its architecture. _____

   5 There needs to be more shopping malls in the Italian capital of Rome. _____

   6 The old buildings of Rome have great historical significance. _____

   7 We need to build more skyscrapers for future generations to live in. _____

   8 The Eiffel Tower was not supported by everyone when it was first built. _____

Throughout history, cities have always changed and grown. As the human population expands, cities need to get bigger, and often taller. Some of the most famous buildings in the world are also the tallest: the 830-metre-high Burj Khalifa in Dubai or the twin Petronas Towers in Kuala Lumpur. However, this rapid development comes at a price. Many old buildings in cities like Kuala Lumpur, Singapore or Shanghai have disappeared, to be replaced by new shopping malls, luxury hotels and skyscrapers. Some places like Dubai have changed out of all recognition in the last 20 years.

However, is this a bad thing? After all, beautiful new skyscrapers and shopping malls do attract tourists. Also, for residents, it is not always safe to live alongside old buildings. In places like Tokyo, there are few very old buildings, most having been destroyed by fires or large earthquakes. In addition, older buildings tend to be small and inconvenient for large cities where overcrowding is already a problem. The cost of maintaining old buildings can also often be huge, especially in cities such as Prague which have extensive old town centres.

On the other hand, some old buildings do have enormous cultural importance. There are few people who would suggest tearing down the ancient buildings of Ancient Rome to build a new shopping mall. Its buildings are simply too precious. They are not only beautiful, but tell us a great deal about how past generations lived. We have to take responsibility for conserving important buildings for future generations to enjoy and learn from.

In conclusion, it is difficult to argue that we should forbid the creation of new buildings. Cities do change and evolve over time. Of course, there are those who don't appreciate modern architecture, but it's worth bearing in mind that when the famous Eiffel Tower of Paris was opened in 1889, it was widely criticized as being 'useless and monstrous'. Each generation creates its own architectural styles, and we should continue that. In short, we need to be able to expand our cities in a way that respects architecture from the past but looks to the future.

2 Match the sentences (1–5) from the article to the paraphrases (a–e). 1 mark for each correct answer.

   1 However, this rapid development comes at a price. _____

   2 Also, for residents, it is not always safe to live alongside old buildings. _____

   3 On the other hand, some old buildings do have enormous cultural importance. _____

   4 We have to take responsibility for conserving important buildings for future generations to enjoy and learn from. _____

   5 In short, we need to be able to expand our cities in a way that respects architecture from the past but looks to the future. _____

   a Tourists may appreciate old buildings, but that doesn't mean they are suitable for citizens.

   b Modernization does have its disadvantages.

c We need to find a compromise between preserving existing architecture and developing cities.

d It is our role to preserve old buildings for our children and grandchildren to appreciate.

e Architecture is a significant part of a nation's identity.

VOCABULARY (10 marks)

3 Complete the sentences with words from the box. 1 mark for each correct answer.

> tower tomb skyscrapers straw affordable
> efficient install green compromise durable

1 Buildings in places where there are hurricanes need to be built of very _____ materials.

2 I work in an office _____ in the city centre.

3 More people would be willing to _____ solar panels on buildings if the cost was lower.

4 It is often more _____ to rent a home than to buy one, especially if you live in a city.

5 The _____ in which he was buried is located in northern Egypt.

6 Originally _____ were buildings which were more than 10 storeys high.

7 There are many advantages to living in a _____ building –energy costs are much lower.

8 This building is not energy _____. It loses a lot of heat through its windows.

9 After much discussion, we reached a _____ on the cost of the new building.

10 Before the use of stone and bricks, many houses were built with mud and _____.

LANGUAGE DEVELOPMENT (10 marks)

4 Complete the sentences with the correct form of the words in brackets. 1 mark for each correct answer.

1 We need to care more about the _____ of our cities. (environment)

2 The building is very _____ – it wasn't designed to be attractive. (function)

3 I work more _____ when I am at home. (efficient)

4 This building is really ugly and seems to _____ everyone who works in it. (depress)

5 If we want to construct skyscrapers, then we should do so _____. (responsible)

6 Lecce in Italy has beautiful baroque-style _____. (architect)

5 Choose the best word (a–c) to complete each sentence. 1 mark for each correct answer.

1 The _____ of old buildings for future generations is very important.

2 The government should have a _____ around the city to prevent urban sprawl.

3 The factory is on the _____ of the city – it takes an hour to get there from the centre.

4 The hotel only has basic _____, such as a 24-hour coffee machine.

1 a compromise	b responsibility	c conservation
2 a green belt	b green	c environmentalism
3 a affordable	b outskirts	c urban sprawl
4 a amenities	b architecture	c functionalism

GRAMMAR FOR WRITING (10 marks)

6 Write an academic synonym for the words and phrases in bold. Use the words in the box. 1 mark for each correct answer.

> calculate   justified   fundamentally   approximately   of no benefit to
> considerable   have a positive impact on   critical   undoubtedly   a great deal

1 It is **really important** that we plan for population increases in our city. _____
2 We urgently need to **figure out** how much it will cost to renovate this building. _____
3 There is, **for sure**, a competition to see who can build the tallest skyscraper. _____
4 It seems there are **loads** of people who want to preserve, historical buildings. _____
5 **Basically**, the problem is that there are not enough places to live. _____
6 It is not clear that the costs of installing solar panels to a building are **worth it**. _____
7 There are **something like** 13 million people living in Tokyo. _____
8 A new skyscraper can **be really good for** the image of a city. _____
9 Destroying old buildings is **a really bad idea for** our national culture. _____
10 You need to invest a **really big** amount of money to create any kind of large building. _____

ACADEMIC WRITING SKILLS (10 marks)

7 Complete the sentences with a word or phrase from the box. 1 mark for each correct answer.

> That is why   For these   In spite of this   These   This

1 Dubai has undergone an extensive construction program over the last two decades. _____, parts of the old city remain unchanged.
2 As well as large earthquakes, Tokyo is also prone to typhoons. _____ reasons, skyscrapers in this city are specially designed to withstand great shocks.
3 The Eiffel Tower in Paris is one of the world's popular tourist attractions. _____ means that there are often very long queues to visit it.
4 The Great Pyramid of Giza was built of very heavy stone. _____ it has survived for several thousand years.
5 Some people believe that we can preserve anything we want through photos or film. _____ people see no problem in replacing old architecture with new buildings.

8 Match sentences (1–5) with the most appropriate follow-up sentence, (a–j). You will not need to use all the follow-up sentences. 1 mark for each correct answer.

1 Some cities have very large populations. _____
2 Skyscrapers should be designed with high safety standards in mind. _____
3 Some cities expand upwards, and some expand outwards. _____
4 We need to reduce the amount of cars in our cities. _____
5 It is better to spend more money on preserving old buildings than creating new ones. _____

a This is because historical buildings are important for our culture.
b This can lead to overcrowding if there are not enough places to live.
c Natural disasters can be a problem if skyscrapers are built in areas where they are common.
d People can enjoy old buildings more.
e Urban sprawl can therefore be a problem.
f This is especially important in places where natural disasters are common.
g The latter can result in urban sprawl if construction continues without limit.
h Pollution from traffic is destroying our buildings.

TOTAL ___/50

Name: .... **Date:** ....

READING (10 marks)

1 Read the article. Match the descriptions (1–4) to the correct paragraph (A–D). 1 mark for each correct answer.

1 Explaining the idea _____
2 Well-known sources of energy _____
3 Using the technology in a real-life situation _____
4 How much power could we create? _____

A Most people are aware that fossil fuels are problematic. Not only are we running out of these resources, they also contribute to global pollution. Equally, most of us are familiar with alternative, renewable power sources, which aim to capture energy from the sun, the wind or even the sea. However, here is one unusual idea you may not have heard of.

B There are well over seven billion people living in the world, and most of us move a lot each day. Scientists have known for a long time that electricity can be produced whenever **pressure** is applied to an object, for example with a footstep. If buildings or streets were equipped with **sensitive** floors, then a large amount of energy could be produced from people's footsteps. This is called *piezoelectricity* (*piezo* comes from the Greek word for 'press').

C One footstep alone cannot **generate** a great deal of power. According to research, a single footstep produces enough energy to keep a small light bulb working for just one second. However, around 28,500 **footsteps** would be enough to **operate** an electric train for one second. If we consider that over three million passengers walk through Shinjuku train station in Tokyo each day, then it is clear that a large amount of power could be generated this way.

D This idea may seem unusual, but some nightclubs in the Netherlands and the UK have already introduced **motion**-sensitive dance rooms. Each floor contains crystals which produce electricity when they are pressed. As you can imagine, the large number of people dancing in these places results in a lot of piezoelectricity, which is then fed to nearby batteries to power the nightclub. Although these 'eco-discos' are not powered completely by alternative means, they have significantly reduced their energy bills.

---

2 Find the words below in the article. Use the context to match them to the meanings (a–f). 1 mark for each correct answer.

1 pressure _____
2 sensitive _____
3 generate _____
4 footstep _____
5 operate _____
6 motion _____

a create
b movement
c the force produced when one object pushes against another
d the action of a person's foot touching the ground
e easily changed or affected by something
f to make something work

VOCABULARY (10 marks)

3 Match the words (1–10) to the definitions (a–j). 1 mark for each correct answer.

1 biofuel _____
2 geothermal energy _____
3 fossil fuels _____
4 carbon footprint _____
5 hydroelectricity _____

6 solar energy _____
7 wind turbine _____
8 carbon neutral _____
9 pollution _____
10 motorized transport _____

a The use of the power of the sun to create electricity
b A measurement of how much carbon dioxide someone produces in their everyday life (for example, by driving, heating their home, etc.)
c Vehicles such as cars, planes, etc.
d Coal, gas or oil, formed underground and made from ancient plants or animals
e Power created from natural heat sources below the ground
f A large machine that creates electricity from moving air
g Power taken from moving water sources, such as rivers
h Fuel made from living things or their waste
i Doing things to reduce your carbon dioxide output by the same amount as you produce it (e.g. by planting trees)
j Damage caused to the air, water, etc. by harmful substances

LANGUAGE DEVELOPMENT (10 marks)

4 Choose the best word (a–c) to complete the collocations. 1 mark for each correct answer.

1 Industrial _____ is one of the leading causes of global warming.
2 Oil _____ is set to decline in the next 50 years.
3 We need to find renewable _____ of energy in order to reduce our dependence on oil and coal.
4 It is possible for cars to run on alternative _____ such as solar energy or natural gas.
5 A nuclear accident would be a major environmental _____.

1 a energy   b pollution   c fuel
2 a production   b fuel   c energy
3 a fuels   b problems   c sources
4 a production   b fuels   c problem
5 a problem   b source   c pollution

5 Write an academic synonym for the verbs in bold. Use the words in the box. 1 mark for each correct answer.

contesting   utilizes   consulting   instigate   diminishing

1 Oil and coal reserves are **decreasing** rapidly. _____
2 There is a need to **start** a plan to reduce our carbon footprint. _____
3 Fewer people are **disagreeing with** the evidence for climate change. _____
4 After **looking at** the report, we agreed with its findings. _____
5 This vehicle **uses** 50% petrol and 50% biofuel. _____

GRAMMAR FOR WRITING (10 marks)

6 Choose the correct relative pronoun. 1 mark for each correct answer.

1 As far as I'm aware, there are few people *who/which* can live without electricity.

2 It wasn't Tokyo, but Sendai *which/where* was hit by the tsunami.

3 I studied Environmental Science *which/when* I was at university.

4 It is not desirable to build wind turbines in areas *where/which* large amounts of people live.

5 Several thousand people, *whose/who* homes were near the new dam, had to be relocated.

7 Complete the phrases to introduce advantages and disadvantages in the texts. 1 mark for each correct answer.

The most [1] o__ __ i__ __ __ advantage of nuclear power is that it is relatively clean. One other [2] i__ __e__e__ __ advantage is that after building a power station, it provides quite cheap energy. Of course, the most [3] s__ __i __ __ __ disadvantage is the risk of nuclear pollution if anything goes wrong.

The [4] d__ __t __ __ __ __ disadvantage of solar power is that you need to invest in a lot of solar panels before you even begin to collect any energy. One other [5] a__ __ a__ __ __ __ disadvantage is that you need to live in a sunny climate for the panels to work successfully.

ACADEMIC WRITING SKILLS (10 marks)

8 Find the mistakes with spelling or a preposition in the sentences and correct them. 1 mark for each correct answer.

1 Most govenment are committed to reducing their carbon footprint.

2 One the most serious problems we face today is the risk of climate change.

3 We need to protect our enviroment for our children.

4 The problem our dependence on oil is that eventually it will run out.

5 Most people nowadays believ that we should not rely so much on fossil fuels.

9 Find the mistakes with countable and uncountable nouns in five sentences and correct them. 1 mark for each correct answer.

1 We need to book accommodations for our holiday next month.

2 This office doesn't have much furniture, does it?

3 More researches have to be conducted before we can make a decision.

4 I lost my luggage at the airport.

5 This computer had a lot of softwares installed.

6 How many equipment do we need to take with us?

7 I really appreciate all the feedbacks you gave me.

8 It's difficult to imagine where all this stuff came from.

TOTAL __/50

Name: .... Date: ....

READING (10 marks)

1 Read the essay. Match the headings (1–4) to the correct paragraph (A–D). 1 mark for each correct answer.

1 Critics of graffiti _____

2 An old art form _____

3 Summarizing the arguments _____

4 In support of graffiti _____

A Graffiti is present in almost every city in the world. The word itself comes from the Italian *graffiato* which means 'scratched'. Indeed, some of the earliest forms of graffiti can be found in ancient Roman sites. The ruins of Pompeii, in southern Italy, contain a large amount of 2000-year-old graffiti which is of great historical significance. However, in the modern world, graffiti has become something negative, and governments spend a great deal of time and money trying to clean it off town and city streets. The question remains: Should graffiti be considered an art form?

B There are some who argue that graffiti is artistic, as it requires as much skill and technique, as any other art form. It may not appeal to everybody, but no one can ever agree on what is beautiful. Graffiti is usually the work of someone trying to express their feelings and personality, and in addition, it usually tries to send a message to other people. This is why some graffiti artists become famous. Indeed, the well-known French graffiti artist, Blek le Rat, has said that he prefers to show his work on the streets, because there it can be seen by as many people as possible.

C There is, of course, an opposing point of view. Perhaps the most important argument against graffiti is that it appears without anyone's permission. In other words, even though nobody asks for graffiti to appear, it does. Art should be about creation, not destruction. However, graffiti may in fact destroy the appearance of a beautiful building, and make whole towns and cities look uglier.

D In conclusion, there seems to be one main question regarding graffiti, and that concerns the artist. Does this person have the right to express his or her feelings in public? On the one hand, yes, artists should be free to express themselves. However, art should not destroy what is already beautiful. In this sense, modern graffiti is not art. It is illegal vandalism, and is no more creative than breaking windows or destroying public phone boxes.

2 Read the essay again. In which paragraphs (A–D) are the ideas below discussed? 1 mark for each correct answer.

1 Graffiti artists do not respect private property. _____

2 You need talent to create graffiti. _____

3 Graffiti can tell us a lot about life in the past. _____

4 Graffiti artists often want to communicate something. _____

5 Graffiti is a crime. _____

6 Graffiti can reduce the overall attractiveness of a city. _____

VOCABULARY (10 marks)

3 Complete the text using words in the box. 1 mark for each correct answer.

sculptures calligraphy banal cynical mechanical fine creative acknowledge aesthetic photography

The ¹ _____ arts are often thought of as paintings or ² _____ which are admired for their beauty, and have no practical use. In other words, we buy this kind of art because of its

³ _____ value, and not because it has any functional use. We ⁴ _____ the ⁵ _____ energy and skill which has gone into making it.

However, can other things be considered as 'art'? What about ⁶ _____, for example – the art of producing beautiful writing? Many ancient Japanese and Chinese texts originally had a functional purpose, but are now considered highly prized works of art. Or ⁷ _____ – can work which relies on a ⁸ _____ device such as a camera really be called 'art'?

Of course, it is common to disagree about what 'art' is. If we think of Marcel Duchamp's *Bicycle Wheel* (which is simply a bicycle wheel placed on a chair) it is easy to be ⁹ _____ and say that the work is simply an ordinary, ¹⁰ _____ object. It's just a bicycle wheel, and therefore not really art. But then again, the artist has used an ordinary bicycle wheel to make us think abut what art is. If this happens, he or she has done their job well.

LANGUAGE DEVELOPMENT (10 marks)

4 Paraphrase the quotes using the words in the box. 1 mark for each correct answer.

> argued   insisted   denied   suggested

1 "The *Mona Lisa* may have been started in 1503 but it probably wasn't finished until 1517."
  He _____ that the *Mona Lisa* may have taken 14 years to finish.

2 "You absolutely must buy this painting – it's beautiful!"
  She _____ that I buy the painting.

3 "No, I didn't break that vase – I wasn't even in the room!"
  He _____ breaking the vase.

4 "Although some people think that graffiti is ugly, my view is that it can be beautiful and exciting to look at."
  She _____ that graffiti could be considered art.

5 Write an adjective to describe the words and phrases in bold. Use the words in the box. 1 mark for each correct answer.

> lifelike   moving   avant-garde   monumental   abstract   expressive

1 I'm sorry, but these paintings are too **modern and original** for my taste – I prefer something a bit more traditional. _____

2 Michelangelo's *David* is a **very big** work of art – the five-metre-high statue can be seen in Florence in Italy. _____

3 The paintings of Gustave Courbet are often very **realistic** – they show real people in ordinary situations doing normal activities. _____

4 I don't understand why **representing ideas and feelings, not real objects** art such as Mark Rothko or Jackson Pollock paintings can be sold for such high prices. _____

5 The film was very **emotional for me** – I don't usually cry in the cinema, but this one left me in tears several times. _____

6 Just look at the child in this painting – she has a really **showing what she thinks and feels** face. _____

GRAMMAR FOR WRITING (10 marks)

6 Match the sentence halves (1–5) with the best ending (a–j). You will not need to use all the endings. 1 mark for each correct answer.

1 Although many people do not like graffiti, _____

2 Michelangelo's sculpture *David* is five metres tall and _____

3 Pablo Picasso was born in Spain in 1881 and _____

4 Calligraphy is the art of writing and _____

5 Henri Cartier-Bresson was a famous photographer, _____

a people not liking graffiti does not make it a crime.

b Picasso's most famous painting is probably Guernica.

c this does not make it a crime.

d Michelangelo's David can be seen in Florence, Italy.

e whose pictures of 20th-century Paris are very well-known.

f this art of writing is popular in many Asian and Arab countries.

g his most famous work is probably Guernica.

h can be seen in Florence, Italy.

i is popular in many Asian and Arab countries.

j Henri and Cartier-Bresson's photographs of 20th-century Paris are very well-known.

7 Complete the sentences using the best phrases in the box. You will not need to use all the phrases. 1 mark for each correct answer.

> was rich and famous   this   it   some graffiti being sold for a lot of money   the *Mona Lisa*
> doesn't like abstract art   was   not   not easy to understand   doesn't

1 Some art is easy to understand, but a lot is _____.

2 I like abstract art, but my wife _____.

3 Many artists were not rich or famous in their own lifetimes, but Picasso _____.

4 The *Mona Lisa* was stolen in 1911, but _____ was returned two years later.

5 Some graffiti art is sold for a lot of money. I know that a lot of people don't agree with _____.

ACADEMIC WRITING SKILLS (10 marks)

8 Complete the paragraph with words in the box. 1 mark for each correct answer.

> these   although   their own   the majority   this
> such labels   for example   that's why   items   In contrast

I would like to discuss whether fashion can be considered 'art'.

Firstly, I believe that the luxury designer products that you can buy in expensive stores should not be called art. [1]_____ products simply encourage people to buy exactly the same things and show how rich they are. [2]_____, these [3]_____ usually come with a logo (often the designer's name) on them, and people who wear clothes with [4]_____ are not expressing [5]_____ personality. They are just copying everyone else.

[6]_____, I think that fashion can be artistic if you dress in a style which reflects your unique personality. [7]_____ can be simply having a hairstyle or wearing a combination of clothes which is different to everyone else's.

[8]_____ most people would like to be truly fashionable, I would say that [9]_____ are afraid to look too different from everyone else. [10]_____ in most cases, what people wear is not 'art'.

TOTAL ___/50

REVIEW TEST 10

Name: .... Date: ....

READING (10 marks)

1 Read the article about the ageing population of Japan. Tick the five questions answered in the article. 1 mark for each correct answer.

   1 What are some of the recent demographic changes in Japan? _____

   2 What social activities do the Japanese enjoy? _____

   3 What percentage of Japan's population can be categorized as elderly? _____

   4 Why does Japan currently have such a large elderly population? _____

   5 Do the Japanese have large pensions when they retire? _____

   6 Does Japan have a large workforce? _____

   7 In what ways is an ageing population a good sign for a country? _____

   8 What are some of the consequences of an ageing population? _____

The population of Japan has increased significantly since the beginning of the 20th century. From a relatively small population of 51 million in 1910, it reached a total of 72 million by 1945. The latter half of the 20th century saw a huge population boom as the country became fully industrialized. By 1970, the population had surpassed 100 million, and it went on to grow by a further 28 million by 2010.

In 2012, however, research showed that the overall Japanese population had started to decrease. Apart from during the year 1945, this was the first time in recent history that this had happened. In 2012, there were one million fewer people living in the country than two years previously.

A closer look at the statistics reveals that Japanese society is clearly ageing, and at a much faster rate than ever before. In 2012, the amount of elderly people (over the age of 65) rose above 30 million for the first time. This meant that elderly people comprised roughly one quarter of the whole population, whereas only 13% were under the age of 14. In this year, Japan officially become one of the 'greyest' countries in the world.

The reasons for this trend are due to Japan's success as a fully developed society. After 1945, as with many countries, there was a 'baby boom', when an increased number of babies were born in a short period due to a more stable and economically favourable environment. By 2010, these 'baby boomers' had begun to leave the workforce, and were officially elderly.

An ageing society can, in theory, be a positive sign. The standard of living tends to be higher in countries which can support an elderly population. In addition, poverty and crime rates tend to be lower. On the other hand, it can cause serious social problems. A large elderly section of society means that more people need health care and there is a smaller section of the population paying taxes to cover the costs of this. This means that over time all governments, including the Japanese government, will increasingly struggle to afford an ageing society.

2 Complete each sentence about the article with a number. 1 mark for each correct answer.

   1 Between 1910 and _____, the Japanese population doubled.

   2 In 2012, Japan's population was approximately _____ million.

   3 In 2012, the elderly population was around _____%.

   4 Children under 14 comprised _____% of the population.

   5 Many people reached retirement age around _____.

VOCABULARY (10 marks)

3 Choose the best word to complete the collocations in each sentence. 1 mark for each correct answer.

1 One of the most important demographic *activities/changes* facing the world today is that the number of people aged 65 or over is increasing faster than at any point in history.

2 Because of the ageing *population/impact*, the government is considering increasing the retirement age from 65 to 70.

3 Japan and Switzerland have the highest average life *expectancy/population*, in the world.

4 The economic *expectancy/impact* of ageing populations will be enormous – the government will be able to collect fewer taxes and will have to spend more on health care.

5 It's important that older people are engaged in social *changes/activities* where they socialize with other people, such as joining clubs or taking part in voluntary work.

4 Complete the sentences with the words in the box. 1 mark for each correct answer.

elderly   shortage   maintain   workforce   decline

1 More than one million people make up the _____ of the British National Health Service. About 150,000 of these are doctors.

2 In many countries, it is common for people to look after their _____ parents at home when they become unable to look after themselves.

3 Many people are worried that there will be a _____ of qualified professionals able to look after old people.

4 In most developed countries, there has recently been a _____ in the number of babies being born – there are fewer than 30 or 40 years ago.

5 We should try to _____ a good standard of living for everyone, young or old.

LANGUAGE DEVELOPMENT (10 marks)

5 Choose the correct word or phrase (a–c) to complete the collocations in each sentence. 1 mark for each correct answer.

1 There is a compulsory _____ age in this country of 65.

2 After working all her life, my grandmother now _____ a pension every month.

3 Despite being 91, my grandfather is in _____ health.

4 Examples of age-_____ diseases include arthritis and Type-2 diabetes.

5 My mother remembers what happened 30 years ago, but her _____ memory is poor.

1 a retirement	b pension	c old
2 a contributes to	b brings back	c draws
3 a happy	b perfect	c advanced
4 a coming	b related	c problem
5 a loss	b later	c short-term

6 Complete the sentences with the correct preposition. 1 mark for each correct answer.

1 The ageing population could, _____ theory, create a crisis in many developed countries.

2 In this essay, I would like to focus _____ some of the reasons why life expectancy has improved in the last 50 years.

3 Many young people find it difficult to identify _____ the problems of elderly people.

4 There are a range _____ theories as to why the population has started to decrease.

5 To sum _____, I would like to discuss the benefits of an older society.

GRAMMAR FOR WRITING (10 marks)

7 Complete the numerical words in each sentence. 1 mark for each correct answer.

1 A large p__ __p__ __t__ __ n of families have more than one child.

2 Only a small m__ __ __r __ __ y of people will live to be over 100 years old.

3 The overwhelming m__ __ __r__t__ of countries are increasing in population.

4 The population has t__ i __ __ __ d in the last 60 years.

5 The number of elderly people needing special care has d__ __ __l __ d.

8 Complete the sentences with the correct language of prediction from the box. 1 mark for each correct answer.

are set to rise   are unlikely to be   are expected to be   may well decrease   is projected to rise

1 The latest figures are looking very positive: unemployment _____ in the next two years, which means fewer people will be without a job.

2 Salaries _____ next year, but only by 1.5%, which does match rises in living costs.

3 The global population _____ from 7 to 8 billion by the year 2050.

4 There _____ so many university students next year, now that education fees have risen.

5 There _____ more elderly people in the next 20 years – in fact 35% of the population will probably be over 65, far more than now.

ACADEMIC WRITING SKILLS (10 marks)

9 Complete the diagram description with the words in the box. 1 mark for each correct answer.

shows   steadily   consequences   analysis   diagram   impact

A This [1] _____ [2] _____ the population of Japan from the late 1800s to the present day. It also shows the projected demographic changes until the year 2100.

B Upon close [3] _____, it can be seen that, apart from a small dip in the 1940s, the population rose [4] _____ until it reached a peak of 128 million in 2010.

C If the population of Japan does decrease as predicted, then this will have great [5] _____ for its society, especially if the proportion of elderly people increases.

D In summary, the Japanese population may well reach a level which is similar to that of more than 100 years ago. This would have a great [6] _____ on society.

10 Match the topics (1–4) to the paragraphs (A–D) of the description. 1 mark for each correct answer.

1 Main implications of the data _____

2 Description and main trends of the data _____

3 Introduction _____

4 General overview _____

TOTAL ___/50

WRITING TASK 1 MODEL ANSWER

How have food and eating habits changed in your country? Suggest some reasons for these changes.

The cuisine of Algeria has changed considerably in recent years. This has affected not only the food, but also the way that it is eaten. This essay will explore some of those changes and suggest reasons for them.

In spite of regional variations, Algeria has a basic list of traditional dishes. These are based on couscous, meat, fish and vegetables, flavoured with spices and mint. Preparation of most traditional meals requires a great deal of time. Historically ingredients were sourced locally or grown at home and were therefore relatively inexpensive.

In recent years this strong tradition of long, slow cooking with fresh ingredients has been challenged. People now buy more foreign foods, including stock cubes, processed cheese, instant coffee and flavoured yoghurts. Many traditional ingredients such as couscous are no longer prepared at home, but manufactured in factories abroad. Fast foods such as ready-made pizzas and burgers are also popular.

There are various reasons for all of these changes. More Algerians now enjoy the convenience of access to large supermarkets, but this also subjects them to advertising from companies who try to persuade them that processed food is a sign of development. Using more convenience food means more time for work, but this work often results in even less time to spend in the kitchen. The availability of cheap restaurants also tempts people away from the traditional family meals around the table.

Modern life certainly seems to be having a major impact on the way Algerians eat nowadays. However, with such a strong tradition of home cooking, many people are determined to reverse trend towards convenience and fast foods and eating outside the home.

ADDITIONAL WRITING TASK 1

How has globalization had an impact on transportation in your country?

_____

_____

_____

_____

_____

_____

_____

_____

WRITING TASK 2 MODEL ANSWER

Outline the various differences between studying a language and studying mathematics. In what ways may they in fact be similar?

Traditionally, subjects such as mathematics and languages are seen as polar opposites. In this essay, studying a language will be compared and contrasted with studying mathematics, both in terms of the subjects themselves and the outcomes of studying them. It will conclude that there are more similarities than customarily expected.

The two subjects clearly differ in many ways. In mathematics, there is usually only one correct answer in a particular situation, whereas linguistically there are many different appropriate ways to express an idea. Similarly, the two subjects are associated with different skills: applying logic in mathematics and intuition in language. Finally, learning a language usually requires interaction with other people, whereas mathematics often needs solitary concentration.

However, there are also similarities between studying the two subjects which at first are less obvious. Both language and mathematics are based on patterns, and students who learns those patterns, whether they are related to equations or grammar, will find it helps them to progress in the subject. In addition, studying both subjects at school level will help the pupil to find a better job, as a basic knowledge of mathematics is needed for the majority of positions and competency in a foreign language such as English is a requirement in many careers. Finally, studying a language and solving mathematical problems are two very effective ways of exercising and developing the brain, so they may benefit the student beyond the acquisition of the actual subject itself.

In conclusion, while studying foreign languages and mathematics may seem to use completely dissimilar skills on the surface, in fact they have a lot in common. Studying both helps provide a well-rounded education.

ADDITIONAL WRITING TASK 2

Describe the similarities and differences between studying at school and attending university in your country.

_____

_____

_____

_____

_____

_____

_____

WRITING TASK 3 MODEL ANSWER

'Avoiding preventable illnesses is the responsibility of individuals and their families, not governments.' Do you agree?

Preventable illnesses are caused by the lifestyle of the patient in question and can lead to incapacity or death. Some of these illnesses are caused by diet and lifestyle, such as heart disease and others are linked to car accidents or work-related injuries. However there are a far larger number of deaths which could have been prevented by access to routine vaccination. It is clearly the responsibility of individuals and governments to work together to reduce the number of preventable deaths. This essay will discuss how the state should support individuals in avoiding preventable illnesses.

When people smoke, eat a fat and sugar-rich diet or live and work in unsafe environments, they are risking their health. There are a number of serious illnesses related to these activities which can reduce the quality of life or shorten it considerably, for example, in the US, at least 200,00 deaths from heart disease and stroke could be prevented each year by changes in diet and lifestyle. It is clear that it is the responsibility of the individual to govern their own lifestyle and, with the benefit of health education, avoid fatty food, dangerous recreational activities and unsafe working environments. However it is the task of the state to provide regulations to protect workers from injury, restrict the sale of harmful substances and give information about healthy lifestyles.

Where preventable illnesses are caused by a lack of access to basic vaccination, the responsibility is that of the government. In 2008, the World Health Organisation estimated that 1.5 million deaths of children under the age of five could have been prevented by basic vaccinations against common childhood illnesses like measles. Governments should provide free immunisation to the general population along with an education programme to underline the seriousness of having children vaccinated. However, it is also the responsibility of parents to ensure that their children are immunised to protect them before they enter education.

In conclusion, while individuals have a basic responsibility to inform themselves about the effect of their lifestyle choices on their health, it is the task of governments to make sure that preventable illnesses are reduced by a combination of vaccination, education and safety regulation.

ADDITIONAL WRITING TASK 3

Should governments fund free healthcare through taxes or should citizens pay themselves with private health insurance?

_____

_____

_____

_____

_____

_____

WRITING TASK 4 MODEL ANSWER

'If children are never exposed to risk, they will never be able to cope with risk.'
Give reasons for and against this statement and give your opinion.

Many people's first reaction to the question of exposing children to risk is to reject the idea. Society is generally shocked to hear of harm to children and adults see it as their role to protect children. Some question, however, whether over-protectioing children from risk is equally harmful in the long term. This essay will explore some arguments in support of exposing children to risk and some that oppose this.

One view is that children are natural risk-takers and protecting them from every minor danger does not allow them to develop fully. Small children learn about the world and how to function within it by taking risks. If they did not do this they would never learn to walk, climb stairs, swim or ride a bicycle. They learn other important lessons as they gain these skills, i.e. that actions have consequences that may sometimes be painful. As children grow older they seek stimulation and challenge and want to explore the limits of risk. By doing this they develop the skill of assessing and controlling hazards, something that will be important for the rest of their lives.

On the other hand, there are many serious threats from which children need to be protected. Although children are learning to assess risk they are not yet competent at this skill and their activities will sometimes need to be restricted by adults. While it is normal for children to sustain minor wounds like bruises and scratches, injuries that will affect the rest of their lives must of course be avoided.

In conclusion, trying to protect children from risks is not only impossible but also prevents them from learning to deal with it in later life. However, adults can take precautions when exposing children to risk by providing play areas that stimulate and offer protection from serious harm.

ADDITIONAL WRITING TASK 4

'The internet provides many conveniences for modern life but these are outweighed by the dangers it presents'. Describe some of the conveniences and dangers of the internet and give your opinion about the statement.

_____

_____

_____

_____

_____

_____

WRITING TASK 5 MODEL ANSWER

Write a description of a process with which you are familiar.

The bread making process

Bread making by hand is less popular than in the past, when it was normal to make your own bread. It is a rather long process, but the results are a significant improvement on commercially produced bread.

Firstly, all the ingredients are weighed. A range of flour types can be used, such as wholemeal, white or rye, but it is imperative that the flour is described as 'strong'. Other ingredients needed are yeast, which can be fresh or dried, and sugar to activate it. In addition, oil, salt, and warm water are required.

There are several important stages in the bread making process, none of which can be omitted. If quick dried yeast is used, this is added directly to the flour in a large bowl with the sugar and salt. A hole is made in the middle of the flour and the water and oil are added. Using a knife, the flour mixture is gradually incorporated into the liquid. After this, the dough is kneaded by hand. This involves stretching the dough and pushing it with the heel of the hand for ten minutes. It is then left to rise in a warm place for about an hour. Next, it is kneaded again for five minutes and shaped, before being left to rise again for another 40 minutes.

Finally the bread needs to be cooked. Before doing this, the top of the dough is brushed with milk or water and can be sprinkled with seeds. Then it is placed in a hot oven for about 40 minutes. The cooked bread should sound hollow when tapped on the bottom. It is advisable to leave the bread to cool for a while before eating.

ADDITIONAL WRITING TASK 5

Write a description of the tanning process (the production of leather).

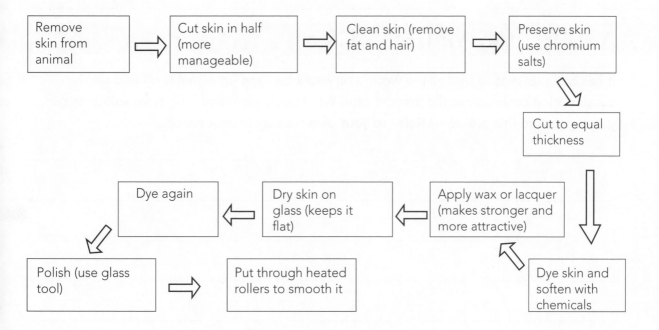

WRITING TASK 6 MODEL ANSWER

Write a report which provides both short- and long-term solutions to an environmental problem. Refer to a specific case study in your report.

<u>Bush fires in southern Australia</u>

Bush fires can be a devastating problem, causing loss of life and property. Whether bush fires are started deliberately or accidentally, the rate that they spread can depend on an area's geography and vegetation. This report will examine some short and long term responses to such fires, with particular reference to southern Australia.

Although the south of Australia has always been prone to bush fires, problems have escalated recently. This region is heavily forested with eucalyptus trees which contain highly flammable oil. As temperatures have risen significantly in Australia due to climate change, the danger of bush fires has increased and many homes and some lives have also been lost.

There are several measures which people who live in bush fire-risk areas can take. On very hot, dry days they should avoid having barbecues or smoking outside. If warned that a fire is approaching, they can spray their houses and surrounding area with water to stop the fire from catching. They should also consider leaving the area if it is safe to do so.

In the longer term, both the country affected and the international community can help. Southern Australia has set up a bush fire monitoring programme with an early warning system, which gives residents time to take protective measures. It is also very important for the local population to be well educated about the risks of fire and how they can protect themselves. Finally, the international community needs to collaborate on reducing activity which may contribute to global warming which is one of the main reasons for the increase in bush fires.

The measures that southern Australia has put in place have saved many lives and could certainly be copied by other countries, provided they have adequate resources. However, one country alone cannot fight global warming, so this responsibility must be shared globally.

ADDITIONAL WRITING TASK 6

It has been estimated that all the world's oil could be used up within forty years if consumption continues at the present rate. What short-term and long-term solutions can you suggest to this problem? Refer to your own country in your report.

_____

_____

_____

_____

_____

_____

WRITING TASK 7 MODEL ANSWER

Which is more important when building or buying a new home: its location or its size?

Constructing or purchasing accommodation is extremely expensive and time-consuming. It is rare to find a house or flat that fits all the criteria of a perfect home, so some compromises may be necessary. First this essay will consider reasons to compromise on location, and then on size. It will conclude that individual circumstances dictate which should take priority when building or buying a home.

There are several reasons why the location of the accommodation is very important. For many people proximity to family or friends is vital. For others, being near shops, work, schools or transport links is as significant. Another reason for favouring location if buying a house is the desire to live in a neighbourhood that is quiet and safe, or exciting and busy, for example.

On the other hand, size is also a key factor for many people. A residence needs to be large enough to accommodate all inhabitants comfortably. Ideally, there should be enough space to allow everyone who lives there to have some privacy and space to work or study. If possible, there should be extra room for any others who arrive or come to live there, such as children, elderly relatives or guests.

Because a location cannot be changed, that must be acceptable, whereas sometimes a house can be expanded if it is too small. However, this is often not possible and in that case cramped accommodation can cause great inconvenience to residents. To decide whether size or location is more important we have to take into consideration the an individual's needs and resources as well as their potential for modifying the accommodation.

ADDITIONAL WRITING TASK 7

Write a report about the form, function and environmental impact of a building that you know well. Make recommendations to improve one of these three aspects.

_____

_____

_____

_____

_____

_____

_____

_____

_____

WRITING TASK 8 MODEL ANSWER

The world is unable to meet its energy needs. What three sources of renewable energy would be most effective in solving this problem in your country? Which is your preferred option?

With an increase in the global demand for energy, there is an urgent need to find alternative sources of power. This essay will consider which forms of renewable energy would be most suitable in solving this problem in the United Kingdom. Because of the geographic and demographic situation of the UK, a combination wind power, hydroelectricity and biomass would be the most effective alternative power sources.

Wind turbines are tall structures with blades that turn when blown by the wind, thus creating energy. They are very clean and the energy is inexhaustible as there will always be wind. They are perfect for the UK because large wind farms can be placed offshore around the island. However, when there is no wind, no energy is produced, so other forms of energy generation would need to complement this.

Hydroelectricity, the generation of energy using water, can take different forms and using the power of the waves around the UK coastline to create energy is an option that needs to be explored further. This energy source can never be exhausted either. However, a distinct disadvantage of this type of hydropower is that it could spoil the attractiveness of the British coastline and affect marine life.

A third option is biomass, which involves burning waste matter to generate steam which can be converted into energy. The most obvious advantage to this is that it effectively disposes of waste while generating electricity. However, a drawback is that biomass creates more greenhouse gases which can increase global warming.

To conclude, a combination of wind and wave power could supply much of the UK's power needs. If biomass techniques develop to eliminate the output of greenhouse gases, it would also be a useful alternative. However, hydroelectricity is probably the best option for providing an inexhaustible power source to deal with the UK's growing energy needs.

ADDITIONAL WRITING TASK 8

Almost half of the world's food is thrown away. Suggest three ways that individuals can reduce the amount of waste they create. Which is the most effective?

_____

_____

_____

_____

_____

_____

WRITING TASK 9 MODEL ANSWER

Fashion, cooking, video games and sport have all been likened to fine art. Choose *one* of these and discuss whether it should be considered fine art, comparable to painting or sculpture.

In order to debate whether fashion should be regarded as fine art, it is first necessary to define 'fashion' in this context. In this essay it will not be discussed in terms of popular trends, but as the design of clothes which are displayed on the catwalk or sold in exclusive shops. This essay will examine similarities and differences between fashion and fine art before deciding whether the former can be considered the same as the latter.

Both artists and fashion designers need to use a mixture of great creativity and a high level of skill in their work. As the famous fashion designer, Zandra Rhodes argued, "The same amount of artistic expression goes into clothes, a piece of pottery or a painting". Some haute couture items can also be very expensive and, like fine art, are only available to the wealthy.

Those who believe that fashion can never be compared to fine art agree with Andy Warhol who says that art is something that "people don't need to have", and we do need clothes to keep us warm. Fashion is much more obviously part of an industry than art is and is therefore usually seen as more commercial. Another argument is that art reflects the history of the period in which it was created. Alice Rawsthorn insists, "Unlike art, fashion rarely expresses more than the headlines of history".

Whether we consider fashion as art or not depends greatly on the definition of art that we use. According to Aristotle, "The aim of art is to represent not the outward appearance of things but their internal significance". In addition, many feel that art should move us and make us think more deeply. The majority of fashion does not do this and therefore can only be classed at most as decorative rather than fine art.

ADDITIONAL WRITING TASK 9

'Cooking may be as much a means of self-expression as any of the arts.' (Fannie Farmer)
Do you agree? Use quotations to support your ideas.

Quotations you can use (in whole or in part) in your essay;

'Cooking requires confident guesswork and improvisation: experimentation and substitution, dealing with failure and uncertainty in a creative way'
(Paul Theroux)

'No one is born a great cook, one learns by doing.'
(Julia Child, *My Life in France*)

'I feel a recipe is only a theme, which an intelligent cook can play each time with a variation.'
(Madam Benoit)

'At the end of the day, it's just food isn't it? Just food.'
(Marco Pierre White)

'Cookery is not chemistry. It is an art. It requires instinct and taste rather than exact measurements.'
(Marcel Boulestin)

'We believe that this world would be happier if it had more good plain cooks.'
(The Good Housekeeping Cook Book)

WRITING TASK 10 MODEL ANSWER

The population pyramids on page 191 show the global population by age in 1950 and 2010 and the projected figures for 2100. Write an essay describing the information and suggesting what the potential global impact could be if the 2100 projections were correct.

The three population pyramids illustrate the changing age distribution of the world's population over the last 65 years and how it is projected to change further by the end of this century.

It is immediately obvious that life expectancy is rising and will probably continue to do so. In 1950 less than eight per cent of the global population was aged over 60 and this has risen to about 12.5 per cent now. This figure is predicted to more than double over the next 85 years. Conversely, we can see that the population under fourteen has decreased greatly, from nearly 35 per cent in 1950 to just over a quarter now, and the trend is projected to continue to less than 18 per cent. We can expect to see a much more even age distribution in the future than in the past or present.

If indeed the population does age in this way, a number of economic and social issues could arise. Assuming people survive much longer but retire at the same age, they will not only be living without paying taxes for longer but will also be drawing their pensions for more years. This means they may have to save much more money while working to pay for their old age. Family life may also be affected. While young and middle-aged parents are looking after their children, the over-sixties may also be kept busy looking after their own elderly parents. Houses may need to be extended to accommodate four or more generations of a family.

If these population projections are accurate, the potential global impact could be huge, as people will need to work much harder, both at work to earn more money to save for pensions and at home caring for older generations.

ADDITIONAL WRITING TASK 10

Describe the three pie charts below and discuss three ways society could be affected by the changes they describe. Refer to the past, present and future.

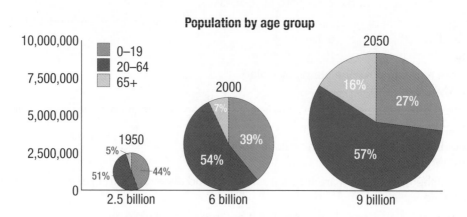

Population by age group

ACKNOWLEDGEMENTS

I would like to thank the editorial team at Cambridge University Press, especially Barry Tadman, Kate Hansford, Carolyn Parsons, Ruth Cox and Caroline Thiriau. I am also hugely grateful to Daryl Fraser who kept me fed, watered and sane throughout the project.
Johanna Stirling

Publisher acknowledgements

The publishers are extremely grateful to the following people and their students for reviewing and trialling this course during its development. The course has benefited hugely from your insightful comments and feedback.

Mr M.K. Adjibade, King Saud University, Saudi Arabia; Canan Aktug, Bursa Technical University, Turkey; Olwyn Alexander, Heriot Watt University, UK; Valerie Anisy, Damman University, Saudi Arabia; Anwar Al-Fetlawi, University of Sharjah, UAE; Laila Al-Qadhi, Kuwait University, Kuwait; Tahani Al-Taha, University of Dubai, UAE; Ozlem Atalay, Middle East Technical University, Turkey; Seda Merter Ataygul, Bursa Technical University Turkey; Harika Altug, Bogazici University, Turkey; Kwab Asare, University of Westminster, UK; Erdogan Bada, Cukurova University, Turkey; Cem Balcikanli, Gazi University, Turkey; Gaye Bayri, Anadolu University, Turkey; Meher Ben Lakhdar, Sohar University, Oman; Emma Biss, Girne American University, UK; Dogan Bulut, Meliksah University, Turkey; Sinem Bur, TED University, Turkey; Alison Chisholm, University of Sussex, UK; Dr. Panidnad Chulerk , Rangsit University, Thailand; Sedat Cilingir, Bilgi University, Istanbul, Turkey; Sarah Clark, Nottingham Trent International College, UK; Elaine Cockerham, Higher College of Technology, Muscat, Oman; Asli Derin, Bilgi University, Turkey; Steven Douglass, University of Sunderland, UK; Jacqueline Einer, Sabanci University, Turkey; Basak Erel, Anadolu University, Turkey; Hande Lena Erol, Piri Reis Maritime University, Turkey; Gulseren Eyuboglu, Ozyegin University, Turkey; Dr. Majid Gharawi and colleagues at the English Language Centre, Jazan University, Saudi Arabia; Muge Gencer, Kemerburgaz University, Turkey; Jeff Gibbons, King Fahed University of Petroleum and Minerals, Saudi Arabia; Maxine Gilway, Bristol University, UK; Dr Christina Gitsaki, HCT, Dubai Men's College, UAE; Sam Fenwick, Sohar University, Oman; Peter Frey, International House, Doha, Qatar; Neil Harris, Swansea University, UK; Vicki Hayden, College of the North Atlantic, Qatar; Ajarn Naratip Sharp Jindapitak, Prince of Songkla University, Hatyai, Thailand; Joud Jabri-Pickett, United Arab Emirates University, Al Ain, UAE; Aysel Kilic, Anadolu University, Turkey; Ali Kimav, Anadolu University, Turkey; Bahar Kiziltunali, Izmir University of Economics, Turkey; Kamil Koc, Ozel Kasimoglu Coskun Lisesi, Turkey; Ipek Korman-Tezcan, Yeditepe University, Turkey; Philip Lodge, Dubai Men's College, UAE; Iain Mackie, Al Rowdah University, Abu Dhabi, UAE; Katherine Mansfield, University of Westminster, UK; Kassim Mastan, King Saud University, Saudi Arabia; Elspeth McConnell, Newham College, UK; Lauriel Mehdi, American University of Sharjah, UAE; Dorando Mirkin-Dick, Bell International Institute, UK; Dr Sita Musigrungsi, Prince of Songkla University, Hatyai, Thailand; Mark Neville, Al Hosn University, Abu Dhabi, UAE; Shirley Norton, London School of English, UK; James Openshaw, British Study Centres, UK; Hale Ottolini, Mugla Sitki Kocman University, Turkey; David Palmer, University of Dubai, UAE; Michael Pazinas, United Arab Emirates University, UAE; Troy Priest, Zayed University, UAE; Alison Ramage Patterson, Jeddah, Saudi Arabia; Paul Rogers, Qatar Skills Academy, Qatar; Josh Round, Saint George International, UK; Harika Saglicak, Bogazici University, Turkey; Asli Saracoglu, Isik University, Turkey; Neil Sarkar, Ealing, Hammersmith and West London College, UK; Nancy Shepherd, Bahrain University, Bahrain; Jonathan Smith, Sabanci University, Turkey; Peter Smith, United Arab Emirates University, UAE; Adem Soruc, Fatih University Istanbul, Turkey; Dr Peter Stanfield, HCT, Madinat Zayed & Ruwais Colleges, UAE; Maria Agata Szczerbik, United Arab Emirates University, Al Ain, UAE; Burcu Tezcan-Unal, Bilgi University, Turkey; Dr Nakonthep Tipayasuparat, Rangsit University, Thailand; Scott Thornbury, The New School, New York, USA; Susan Toth, HCT, Dubai Men's Campus, Dubai, UAE; Melin Unal, Ege University, Izmir, Turkey; Aylin Unaldi, Bogaziçi University, Turkey; Colleen Wackrow, Princess Nourah bint Abdulrahman University, Riyadh, Saudi Arabia; Gordon Watts, Study Group, Brighton UK; Po Leng Wendelkin, INTO at University of East Anglia, UK; Halime Yildiz, Bilkent University, Ankara, Turkey; Ferhat Yilmaz, Kahramanmaras Sutcu Imam University, Turkey.

Special thanks to Peter Lucantoni for sharing his expertise, both pedagogical and cultural.

Special thanks also to Michael Pazinas for writing the Research projects which feature at the end of every unit. Michael has first-hand experience of teaching in and developing materials for the paperless classroom. He has worked in Greece, the Middle East and the UK. Prior to his current position as Curriculum and Assessment Coordinator for the Foundation Program at the United Arab Emirates University he was an English teacher for the British Council, the University of Exeter and several private language institutes. Michael is also a graphic designer, involved in instructional design and educational eBook development.

Photos

p.8: (1) © Eric Limon/Shutterstock; p.8: (2) © szefai/Shutterstock; p.8: (3) © Steven Vidler/Eurasia Press/Corbis.

All other video stills are by kind permission of © Discovery Communication, LLC 2014.

Dictionary

Cambridge dictionaries are the world's most widely used dictionaries for learners of English. Available at three levels (Cambridge Essential English Dictionary, Cambridge Learner's Dictionary and Cambridge Advanced Learner's Dictionary), they provide easy-to-understand definitions, example sentences, and help in avoiding typical mistakes. The dictionaries are also available online at dictionary.cambridge.org. © Cambridge University Press, reproduced with permission.

Corpus

Development of this publication has made use of the Cambridge English Corpus (CEC). The CEC is a multi-billion word computer database of contemporary spoken and written English. It includes British English, American English and other varieties of English. It also includes the Cambridge Learner Corpus, developed in collaboration with Cambridge English Language Assessment. Cambridge University Press has built up the CEC to provide evidence about language use that helps to produce better language teaching materials.

Typeset by Integra

fit
from the
start

How to Prevent Childhood
Obesity in Infancy

Alvin N. Eden, **MD** · Barbara J. Moore, **PhD**
Adrienne Forman, **MS, RDN**

DATE DUE

PRINTED IN U.S.A.